# *The Amazing Bugattis*

GW00992027

*THE*
**DESIGN**
*COUNCIL*

First edition published in the
United Kingdom 1979 by
The Design Council
28 Haymarket, London SW1 4SU
to coincide with the occasion of the
Royal College of Art's exhibition
'The Amazing Bugattis' presented by
*The Observer* in association with
Moët & Chandon and the Bugatti
Owners' Club, 8 October to
18 November 1979

Designed by Betty Dougherty

Printed and bound in the United Kingdom by
Jolly & Barber Ltd, Rugby

Distributed by
Heinemann Educational Books Ltd
22 Bedford Square, London WC1B 3HH

British Library CIP Data
The Amazing Bugattis
  1. Bugatti, Ettore  2. Bugatti, Jean
  3. Businessmen – Italy – Biography
  4. Bugatti, Rembrandt  5. Bugatti, Carlo
  I. Haslam, Malcolm  II. Design Council
  338.7'62'922220922   TL140.B8

ISBN 0 85072 104 0

# Contents

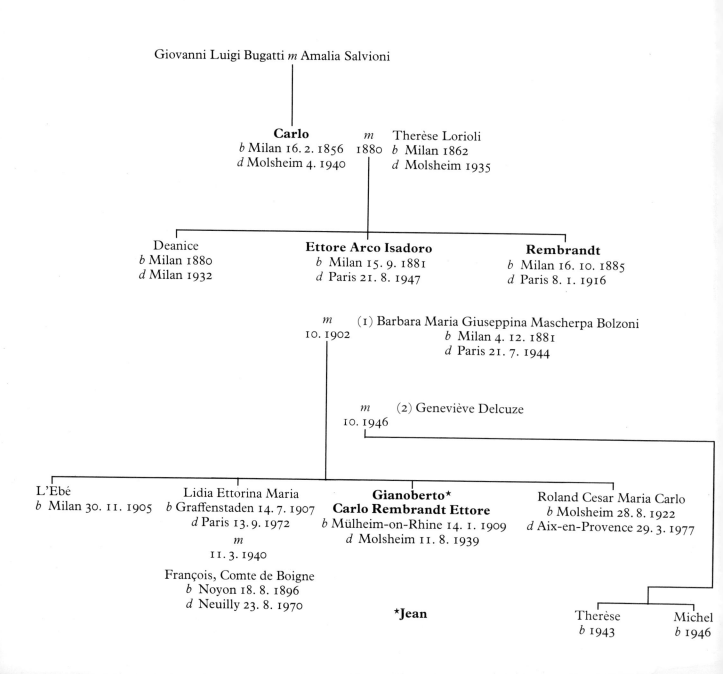

Giovanni Luigi Bugatti *m* Amalia Salvioni

**Carlo**    *m*    Thèrèse Lorioli
*b* Milan 16. 2. 1856   1880   *b* Milan 1862
*d* Molsheim 4. 1940      *d* Molsheim 1935

Deanice      **Ettore Arco Isadoro**      **Rembrandt**
*b* Milan 1880    *b* Milan 15. 9. 1881    *b* Milan 16. 10. 1885
*d* Milan 1932    *d* Paris 21. 8. 1947    *d* Paris 8. 1. 1916

*m*    (1) Barbara Maria Giuseppina Mascherpa Bolzoni
10. 1902      *b* Milan 4. 12. 1881
       *d* Paris 21. 7. 1944

*m*    (2) Geneviève Delcuze
10. 1946

L'Ebé    Lidia Ettorina Maria    **Gianoberto***    Roland Cesar Maria Carlo
*b* Milan 30. 11. 1905   *b* Graffenstaden 14. 7. 1907   **Carlo Rembrandt Ettore**   *b* Molsheim 28. 8. 1922
   *d* Paris 13. 9. 1972   *b* Mülheim-on-Rhine 14. 1. 1909   *d* Aix-en-Provence 29. 3. 1977
     *m*    *d* Molsheim 11. 8. 1939
     11. 3. 1940

François, Comte de Boigne
*b* Noyon 18. 8. 1896
*d* Neuilly 23. 8. 1970

***Jean**

Thèrèse    Michel
*b* 1943    *b* 1946

# Introduction

## Malcolm Haslam

*Three generations of the Bugatti family – from left to right, Ettore, his son Jean, and Carlo the grandfather – in front of the villa at Molsheim in about 1937.*

At first sight it is difficult to see any common link between the furniture, bronzes and motor cars described and illustrated in this book, except the surname of their creators. It would be impossible for any critic to postulate a 'Bugatti style'. On the other hand, three generations of the same family are likely to have a degree of continuity in their mental attitudes, and what one hopes to find in their various enterprises is a shared motivation. Then it may be possible to define a 'Bugatti identity'.

The Royal College of Art, London, is an appropriate location for an exhibition of work by the Bugattis. The combination of widely different media under the same roof is characteristic of the establishment. Every summer, when the students of the college exhibit their work, there is sculpture on show together with furniture in exotic materials and of outlandish design, and generally there are also one or two motor vehicles of advanced conception. This is not coincidence. The achievements of Carlo Bugatti (1856–1940) and his sons Ettore (1881–1947) and Rembrandt (1885–1916) collectively represent an attitude to art that developed round the turn of the century, and on which the teaching at the Royal College has come to be largely based. It is an attitude where no great distinction is drawn between fine and applied art, where the handling of materials is as important as any aesthetic philosophy, and where the solution of problems becomes as significant a part of the creative process as personal expression. There is far less emphasis at the college on traditional style than there is on the two qualities from whose union so much of the Bugatti achievement springs – observation and invention. 'In a short while, just by looking at the machine, I had grasped all the intricacies of its mechanism,' wrote Ettore Bugatti (quoted by Hugh Conway elsewhere in this book), '. . . I very quickly thought of modifications . . . some of them proved to be valid. . . .'

It is easy to imagine that Carlo Bugatti would have been a contented student at the Royal College of Art as it has

5

*Carlo Bugatti (1856–1940) photographed with examples of his remarkable furniture, probably during the 1890s. His long frock coat and boater-style hat are also to his own, individualistic design.*

become today. But he felt nothing but scorn for art schools after his own experience at the Brera Academy in Milan; in later life he would not even acknowledge his attendance at the Brera, although Ettore studied sculpture there. The courses at the Brera Academy in the second half of the nineteenth century had been unchanged for eons – the classical orders, drapery and the nude formed a curriculum as dull as it was conservative. The symbolist painter Giovanni Segantini, who studied at the Brera at the same time as Carlo Bugatti and who married his sister Luigia in 1881, wrote: 'The art of the past required the study of the nude, statues, drapery and the antique, and for this a school was necessary. But nowadays a young artist must study in the fields, in the streets, in the theatres, and in the cafés – and there he does study.' Many artists of the later nineteenth century were impressed by the speed with which yesterday was forgotten, and they wanted to survey their own world with eyes unprejudiced by the accumulated inheritance of the past.

The situation of the young artist in Italy after the successful completion of *risorgimento* was ambivalent. He felt the need to be modern. Mazzini had announced an intellectual movement 'more stirring, more *initiating* than all French and German *systems* have been or ever will be'. But simply because of this antipathy towards the cultures of the former occupying powers, France and Austria, Italian art struggled along, usually at least a decade behind developments elsewhere in Europe. The *macchiaioli* painters were never abreast of the French Impressionists, and nearly half a century later when Marinetti brought the Futurist artists to Paris they felt compelled to repaint their canvases in the light of Cubism. There were, too, round the neck of every young Italian artist the twin millstones of antiquity and the Renaissance, and often their modernism consisted merely of throwing off this burden. The consequent feeling of weightlessness is sometimes reflected in their art. 'A roaring motor car . . .', wrote Marinetti in the Futurist manifesto (1909), 'is more beautiful than the *Victory of Samothrace*'. But the Futurists did not create motor cars.

In Milan, avant-garde activities during the 1860s and 1870s were the preserve of a movement called '*la scapigliatura*' ('dishevelledness', 'untidiness') which included writers, musicians and artists. Their meeting-place was the *Famiglia Artistica*, founded in 1873, where

*Rembrandt Bugatti (1885–1916) working on a sculpture of
an elephant at the Antwerp Zoological Gardens in about 1913
during the happiest period of his tragically short life.*

exhibitions and lectures took place. Most of their aesthetic principles were derived from Baudelaire and embraced, among other things, a Sardanapalian romanticism which suggests a source for the Near-Eastern style of Carlo Bugatti's furniture. As Philippe Garner points out in his contribution to this book, the Near East and all things Arabian had taken hold of the French artistic imagination in the middle of the nineteenth century. In many respects the Milanese avant-garde was inspired by ideas that had been developed elsewhere in Europe earlier in the century but, because of their city's proximity to Paris and London, Milanese artists had the opportunity to gain first-hand experience of recent developments north of the Alps. Moreover, Milan, having won its independence earlier than most Italian cities, had exploited its geographical position to become a thriving centre of commerce and industry. A population of 320,000 in 1881 had grown to 560,000 by 1906. There had quickly emerged a bourgeoisie that regularly travelled by train to the other great cities of Europe and returned home, not only with commercial contracts, but also with artistic ideas. Carlo Bugatti went to Paris every year; another widely travelled Milanese was Vittore Grubicy (1851–1920) who took up painting at 33 when on a visit to his friend the painter Anton Mauve in Holland. Grubicy was a leading light in Milanese artistic circles, and a close friend of Giovanni Segantini; he brought to Lombardy not only the theories of Impressionism and Neo-Impressionism but also the ideas of John Ruskin.

It is Ruskin's attitude to what may be termed the morality of art that is reflected in the work of all the Bugattis, and which gives their heterogeneous activities an aspect in common. *Modern Painters*, Ruskin's first major work, had called on the artist to seek inspiration in nature. From his examination of the great Gothic monuments Ruskin had developed the thesis that the value of art depended primarily on the society that produced it, and particularly on the social conditions of the producers. He had elevated the individuality of the medieval artisan and decried the uniform, mechanical contrivance of modern industrial art. In Milan during the second half of the nineteenth century there were still numbers of house-workers, individual artisans working at home in metal, wood and leather. Indeed, the thriving furniture manufacture of the Milan district was carried on in this

way. Carlo Bugatti's furniture was made in his own workshops, where he and later his sons worked with their own hands, but there would have been no lack of skilled craftsmen from whom he could have received instruction and assistance; probably some of the metal and leatherwork was carried out by these craftsmen in their own homes and then brought to the Bugatti workshops for assembly. The high standard of craftsmanship found in Bugatti furniture (which is somewhat lacking in the pieces made after 1905 by the De Vecchi concern) was noticed by a reviewer of the Italian Exhibition in London in 1888; writing in the *Journal of Decorative Art* he claimed Bugatti as a true disciple of John Ruskin.

Ettore Bugatti would have benefited as much as his father from the tradition of craftsmen working in their own homes which still prevailed in Milan during the second half of the nineteenth century. The situation there (and it was the same in Turin) was ideal for the development of automobile engineering. House-workers in Milan used lathes and other machine tools powered by electricity, so that the various processes involved would have been comparatively quick, simple and cheap. In 1883 Milan had become one of the first cities in Europe to use electricity for street lighting, tramcars and industrial power; the Italian Edison Company had built an electricity generating plant on the River Adda where some of the dynamos from the old Holborn Viaduct station in London had been installed.

The old dye-works at Molsheim where Ettore established his workshops in 1909 were quickly transformed into something resembling a country estate rather than a motor car factory. 'Le Patron' was enthusiastic about horses and for many years the stables and paddocks dominated the workshops and drawing offices. The workforce consisted almost entirely of skilled craftsmen – 'turners and fitters, millers, smiths and the like', wrote Friderich, Ettore's chief mechanic who was responsible for gathering the team together. Writing in *The Autocar* in 1928, W. F. Bradley described a visit to the Bugatti establishment at Molsheim, and he declared: 'John Ruskin's soul would have been delighted at this example of the artist-artisan; of the engineer who seeks to vent his artistic temperament in terms of mechanics . . . of the man who has happily combined an artistic home with production methods and who has succeeded in

ransmitting this joyous creative spirit to all those who
labour with him.'

The Ruskinian essence of Rembrandt Bugatti's
sculpture is less definable. Perhaps it amounts to no more
than a reverence for nature – a rather idealised nature
where the animals are docile and dignified. The artist's
suicide in January 1916, not long after Italy had entered
the First World War, suggests his inability to accept the
cruelty and competition that characterised Europe at that
time. His animals in bronze, sculpted from models in the
Antwerp Zoo, have been removed from any struggle for
survival, as Rembrandt was finally to remove himself. Two
of his father's friends probably helped to form this
sensitive soul. One was the Russian sculptor Prince
Troubetzkoy, who would not only have stimulated
Rembrandt's instinct to model, but also would have
imbued him with Tolstoyan ethics; Troubetzkoy was an
acquaintance of the great Russian writer and introduced
him on one occasion to the Bugatti household. The other
important influence on the young Rembrandt's mind must
have been his uncle, the painter Giovanni Segantini.
Rembrandt's first sculpture, of three cows led by a
peasant, sounds like a plastic representation of a typical
Segantini subject. The painter died in 1899 and it had only
been in his last few years that he had created the strange
symbolist pictures that ensured him a place in the history
of modern art. Before then he had painted the peasants of
Northern Italy, often with their cows or sheep; humans
and animals alike are represented as humble, but dignified,
victims of their cruel environment. Many times must
Rembrandt as a boy have accompanied his family on
outings from Milan to visit Aunt Luigia and Uncle
Giovanni who lived in the Brianza by Lake Como. The
simplicity and serenity of their rural household would have
contrasted in Rembrandt's mind with his family's bustling
home in crowded Milan.

From the Ruskinian ideals that permeate the work of
the Bugattis there springs a significant limitation to their
achievements. Because they were more concerned with the
methods and morals of their respective enterprises than
with cultural developments in society, to some extent they,
like Ruskin, lost touch with the world in which they lived.
The originality – even *bizarrerie* – of Carlo Bugatti's
furniture is irrefutable, but his work was never really
modern. The Art Nouveau style of the furniture he

*Ettore Bugatti (1881–1947) at the age of 43 pictured beside
his automobile masterpiece, the Type 35 2-litre racing car, at
its first appearance in the 1924 Lyons Grand Prix.*

9

*Jean Bugatti (1909–1939), Ettore's elder son, aged about 21, with a Bugatti saloon made for his sister Lidia. He strongly influenced the design of the later Bugatti cars and their coachwork.*

exhibited at Turin in 1902 was more of a nod in the direction of a fashion that by then was very much on the way out. The future lay with the simple, cheap furniture that was already being developed in Germany, the USA and Scandinavia. Nor do Rembrandt Bugatti's bronzes represent the mainstream of modern sculpture during his lifetime. His compatriot and near contemporary Umberto Boccioni (1882–1916) was much more of a pioneer; his 'Unique Forms of Continuity in Space' dates from 1913. By the time of Rembrandt's death in 1916, Tatlin had started work on his 'Constructions'.

At first sight it is more difficult to see how one can argue that Ettore Bugatti's achievement was not an integral part of the development of the modern motor car. He and his son Jean pioneered details of mechanical design and styling that were widely adopted. But in one respect Ettore, too, suffered from his adherence to Ruskinian principles. If, as W. F. Bradley wrote in 1928, Molsheim would have delighted the soul of John Ruskin because of Ettore's success 'in transmitting the joyous creative spirit to all those who labour with him', this did not prevent the workforce in 1936 from joining in the spontaneous strikes and sit-ins over pay and conditions which swept through French industry. 'Le Patron' was, like Ruskin, paternalistic. What would the modern union negotiator make of his system of extra payments to those employees who could prove that they had saved money? Blinded by high principles, Ettore failed to see the direction in which society was moving. He designed and manufactured beautiful machines for the rich few, unable to understand that the motor car was essentially a popular art form. The future lay not with Bugatti or Ferrari, but with Henry Ford and André Citroën.

Of course it would be outrageous to *blame* the Bugattis for not being conscious of the needs of modern, democratic society, needs that in any case few modern artists have fulfilled. But the problem that contributed to John Ruskin's eventual madness, and which beset every artist following his precepts, was how to make art alive and meaningful to everybody, how to recapture that universality which seems to have characterised the religious art of the Middle Ages. Giovanni Segantini expressed the dilemma thus: 'At the present day a universal and popular feeling for art does not exist. A few solitary artists who create genuinely personal works may be found scattered in different parts of the civilised world. These solitary precursors have a limited number of admirers; they are striking personalities, and their art remains highly aristocratic. . . . We have come forth by revolution from a world whose ancient institutions were in harmony with its beliefs and ideals, and consequently with the arts; and we now find that the latter are unsuited to our tastes, and to our modern life, especially in the centres of the highest culture, and we reject old formulas without having even imagined new ones capable of being substituted for them and suited to the new life.' It was this feeling of frustration at being unable to create an art that was appreciated beyond the confines of a small clique which drove many artists throughout Europe to remove painting from the shackles of photographic realism in order to make their art more profound. 'In the future,' wrote Segantini, 'when we shall have passed through the period of material transformation and compromise, from the new form of society a new and more vital form of art will be evolved. Literature, music and painting will no longer be slaves and prostitutes, but powerful and noble rulers, and they will form the Trinity of the spirit. . . . Art should occupy the vacuum left in us by the decline of religious feeling; the art of the future must appear like the science of the soul, for a work of art is its revelation.' Such visionary language is obscure, but one remembers that Segantini was one of the few nineteenth-century artists applauded by Kandinsky in *Concerning the Spiritual in Art*.

Avant-garde art of the twentieth century has been incomprehensible to most people. Segantini's vision has not been realised and still today art 'remains highly aristocratic'. There was, however, another way out of the dilemma. Many artists of the late nineteenth century turned their attention to the design and manufacture of the things people use. This is what Carlo Bugatti did. To produce the mechanical objects with which man increasingly surrounded himself meant combining the talents of artist and engineer. This is what Ettore Bugatti did. That the art of the Bugattis did not, however, go beyond a much larger circle of admirers than that which patronised painting and sculpture may, once again, be laid at Ruskin's door, for he condemned mass production. He could not have foreseen that in the modern world more people would want to have the pleasure of owning their own car than would have the time, ability or inclination to enjoy making it for themselves. So perhaps the Model T Ford, the Volkswagen, the 2CV Citröen and the Mini are solutions to the problem of universalising art in the age of the consumer society.

Whether one regards as more significant the Bugattis' successes or failures in overcoming the dilemma of art in the modern world, their creations are there to be enjoyed. Their efforts need no further justification than their achievements. We can only be grateful to an Italian family that has visually enriched the twentieth century with such original and delightful work.

A bedroom created for the London home of Lord Battersea by
Carlo Bugatti in about 1900. Carlo has given free rein to his
love of the theatrical in this opulent scheme, and it is worth
remembering that his furniture was intended to be seen against
such backgrounds.

# Carlo Bugatti 1856-1940

Philippe Garner

Carlo Bugatti was truly the child prodigy of the decorative arts in Italy in the last decades of the nineteenth century. His is the only name from Italy to have attained international recognition at a time when the decorative arts were dominated by British theorists and the most fertile centres of creativity were in France, Belgium, Germany/Austria and the United Kingdom. A curious parallel can be drawn between the isolated emergence, in Italy, of Bugatti and the emergence from the other principal Latin country of Europe, Spain, of another equally eccentric and individualistic talent, Antonio Gaudi, who created in Barcelona his own baroque and fantastic version of Art Nouveau. Both artists are regularly hailed as isolated geniuses, a description that should perhaps be treated with caution since each in his own way was very much a reflection of his era. Their achievement was in taking those few extra steps stylistically, into territories that, with considerable flair and inspiration, they made their own.

Born on 16 February 1856 in Milan, Carlo Bugatti was at least a second-generation artist. His father, Giovanni Luigi, was a sculptor with interests in architecture and in certain scientific pursuits. He is best remembered for sculpting ornamental chimney-pieces and for his single-minded pursuit of a dream of creating a mechanism to prove his theory of perpetual motion. Into this dream he poured a great deal of money, and he took it, unrealised, to his grave. In his single-mindedness, if nothing else, Carlo was his father's son.

Both Carlo himself and subsequent commentators, eager to uphold the idea of the spontaneous nature of his genius, have tended to play down his formal artistic training, preferring the image of the self-taught Renaissance man. Rossi-Sacchetti, in his 1907 monograph, describes Carlo's tastes as '. . . inspired by his instinct and not by the rules of a school'. In the text of her unpublished biographical essay on her grandfather, L'Ebé Bugatti reminds us that

Carlo was nicknamed 'The Young Leonardo' for the diversity of his creative drive. The late 1870s, nonetheless, found Carlo as a student at the Brera, Milan's school of art, where he made the acquaintance of a fellow student who was to become his brother-in-law, the painter Giovanni Segantini. His time as a student in Milan was followed by a period of study at the Beaux Arts in Paris. His initial enthusiasm was for architecture and, although no record has been found of any of his architectural schemes being carried through to construction, he evidently enjoyed the creative exercise of building architectural maquettes. Documented examples, which include a curious pyramid-shaped war memorial and an arab-style house, bear witness to the originality of his approach. He finally devoted his

appearance, and he devised for himself a highly individual mode of dress. A stomach weakness, causing an aversion to conventional tightly waisted garments, led him to devise a novel style of trouser, tailored on the principle of workmen's dungarees, rising high above the waistline and reaching the shoulder-blades at the back, with the flaps joined by very short braces. Over this he wore a meticulously tailored frock coat, cut edge to edge at the front and falling straight to a right angle at the knee. Horizontally cut openings led to deep pockets in the lining; the upright, four-centimetre-high collar was linked at the front by a short gold chain at each end of which was a glass cat's eye set in gold. The fine woven cloth would, according to its tone, reflect the season. The outfit was completed by a boater-style hat in fine straw for everyday wear, and in felt for special occasions.

Such was the appearance of the spirited character who in the 1880s found his way into Milanese intellectual and artistic society, where many doors were doubtlessly opened for him by Segantini, who had married Carlo's sister Luigia in 1880. He became acquainted with the sculptors Prince Paul Troubetzkoy, Ercole Rosa and De Grandi, composers Giacomo Puccini and Leoncavallo, the librettist and poet Illica and the publisher Ricordi. This period saw the birth of three children to Carlo and his wife Thérèse Lorioli, whom he had married in 1880–a daughter Deanice, born in 1880, and two sons who were both destined to achieve fame in their own right, Ettore, born in 1881, and Rembrandt, born in 1885.

Carlo's initial approach to furniture was to regard it as a branch of artistic creativity, and he learned to work all the novel materials he chose to employ so that the end product could be truly his own creation. His earliest work in this vein would seem to be the bedroom suite conceived as a wedding gift to his sister and to which Segantini added the painted decoration. Public records detail the establishment in 1888 of a more commercial workshop at 6 Via Castelfidardo, Milan, for the production of furniture.

L'Ebé gives what must presumably be a subsequent address of the workshops when she describes her grandfather's departure from Milan to Paris in about 1904. The attractions of other media, the pressures of running a workshop for the costly production of his hand-crafted furniture, perhaps also the feeling that he had explored to the full the possibilities of his personal style, and the lure

studies to cabinet-making and, although his gifts were multifarious, it was his furniture that brought him international renown and ensured his posthumous fame. Other aspects of his work were overshadowed, and of these the most unjustly neglected have been his designs for silver, a material that attracted him late in his creative life but in which, with his inimitable *brio*, he created works that are today little known but of a brilliance that deserves closer scrutiny.

The picture we have of Carlo Bugatti, built up from a composite of photographs, self-portraits and memories, is of a man of medium height with pale blue eyes and a fine pale blonde beard with which he toyed constantly. His eccentricity was cultivated to a fine degree in his personal

*Opposite: Carlo in later life.*
*Below: Carlo's portrait in oils of*
*his wife, Thérèse Lorioli.*

*Below: a silver teapot and tea service made by*
*A. A. Hébrard to Carlo Bugatti's designs in about 1908 or*
*1910. They are typical of the high-quality wares produced to*
*Carlo's extraordinary designs on insect or grotesque animal*
*themes during this brief period of activity in Paris.*

of Paris combined to encourage Carlo to cede his business at 13 Via Marconia, Milan, to the firm of De Vecchi. He found an atelier in Paris in the rue Jeanne D'arc, 13ème, where he resumed his painting and sculpture. He did not however abandon his interest in furniture and, indeed, accepted various commissions, relying for help on local craftsmen. The stores Maison Dufayel and Bon Marché were among his patrons during this period, before his retirement around 1910 to Pierrefonds, near the forest of Compiègne. This Paris period was most significant for

Carlo's venture into *orfèvrerie*, with exhibitions chez Hébrard and at the Salons des Artistes Décorateurs.

The move from Paris was made for the sake of Carlo's wife, whose frail health supported with difficulty life in the metropolis. Carlo filled his time with painting and sculpture and during the years of the First World War became Mayor, winning considerable local respect for his courage under German occupation. He bravely helped the wounded, concealing them as he stayed on in the village alone on the two occasions when Pierrefonds was

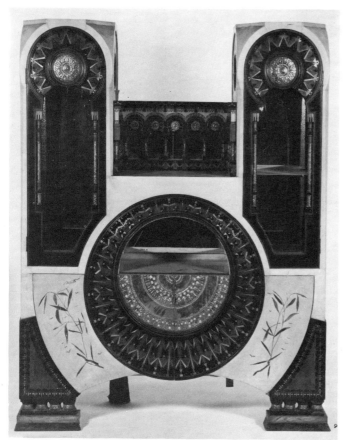

*A vitrine and table from a suite of furniture sold at Sotheby's Belgravia in July 1974. They are characteristic of Carlo's work during the later 1890s, with a growing tendency towards stylisation and an increasing use of vellum.*

evacuated in the face of the German advance. L'Ebé tells two significant stories that give an idea of the man's fibre. She records his bravery in making no effort to conceal a sculpture on which he was working in which the proud *coq gaulois*, its wings extended, was crushing in its powerful claws the peaked helmet that symbolised the oppressor. She also tells of how he patiently restored bones, thrown into the open by the shelling of the Pierrefonds graveyard, to the dignity of their resting place.

In 1932 Carlo lost his daughter Deanice and three years later, in 1935, he was further distressed by the death of his wife. Left alone, he decided to move to Molsheim in about 1937 to be near his elder son Ettore and his grandchildren. Mourning the death in August 1939 of his beloved grandson Jean, and with his spirit finally broken by the declaration of war and the closure of his son's factory, Carlo Bugatti died in April 1940 at the Château St Jean, Dorlisheim, Bas-Rhin. The memories of his courage during the First World War had not perished, and he was accorded full military honours at his funeral. Four soldiers carried his coffin, another followed carrying the tricolour of his adopted country, and a small detachment sounded the last post.

However individual, Carlo Bugatti's *oeuvre* can be better understood and appreciated if seen within the context of prevalent ideology and fashion. Though his was an extremely personal style, comparisons can be made that help to shed light both on Bugatti and on the richly creative period in which he worked. The late nineteenth century saw the formulation of new ideas on design and decoration that were to find a powerful expression in the international Art Nouveau movement at the turn of the century. The background to the evolution of Art Nouveau was complex and diverse, and consequently its final manifestation adopted several distinct, and at times almost opposite, guises. Above all there was felt to be a need to create a new style, divorced from the slavish and misguided subservience to eighteenth-century styles that had characterised so much commercial design during the nineteenth century. Industrialisation had led to a decline in creative inspiration and there was as yet no alliance between art and industry. The new ideologies were formulated in England, and in John Ruskin and William Morris found preachers whose gospel spread through most of Europe and to the United States of America. They demanded truth to materials and a reappraisal of the importance of the role of the craftsman as opposed to that of the machine. Nature was hailed as the finest source of inspiration in the creation of decorative motifs and in the appreciation of structure and proportion. Japanese art, with its purity of line and reduction to essential forms, was a primary shaping force. The more decorative aspects of Japanese art had already inspired the Aesthetic Movement in England before the more intellectual qualities of this new import influenced the designers of the Art Nouveau movement.

Despite the importance of functionalism as an element of the new ideology, it became above all a pursuit of style. Historicism was rejected and Nature adopted, at first in the

*This walnut writing cabinet by Carlo, made in walnut inlaid with ebony, brass and pewter by De Vecchi in about 1905, is in a more restrained style that echoes the decorative work of Owen Jones.*

*Opposite:* the bed and shelf designed as a wedding gift from Carlo to his sister and Segantini, who married in 1880. This is the earliest known example of Carlo's furniture and displays all the characteristics of his early work.

*Below: a cabinet, heavily inlaid in metal and wood with vellum and metal panels, designed by Carlo as part of a complete room furnishing in the late 1890s.*

tight, neo-gothic formulations of designers such as the French architect Viollet le Duc or the English artist/theorists Owen Jones and Christopher Dresser; finally in the full organic fluidity of high Art Nouveau as it emerged around 1900, finding its most sculptural expression in the work of such artists as Hector Guimard and Victor Horta.

Carlo Bugatti's furniture reflects many of these trends. The structural restraint and naturalistic or eclectic decoration of his earliest works evolved towards a greater boldness of form and sophistication of detail. It is significant that a contemporary commentator, writing in *The Cabinet Maker & Art Furnisher*, (IX, 1888–9), was reminded by Carlo's work of 'some of the highly original forms that used to come from the pencil of Christopher Dresser'. By 1902 and his designs for the Turin exhibition, Carlo's previous experiments were superseded by a new, liberated style and the dominant feature was a sculptural freedom and organic vigour that was at once totally personal yet perfectly integrated with the Art Nouveau movement. From the naturalistic or pseudo-arabic inlays of his early work, Carlo's decorative style matured as he mastered the art of flat pattern making by the stylisation of plant and insect motifs. A writing cabinet in the Bethnall Green Museum, London, made to Carlo's design by De Vecchi around 1905, is inlaid with a decoration of stylised flowers that can be seen as a disciplined, yet formal, exercise in Art Nouveau, while at the same time inviting comparison as the direct descendant of the graphics of Dresser or Jones, whose *The Grammar of Ornament* of 1856 was perhaps the most influential contribution to the study of decoration in the second half of the nineteenth century.

If Carlo's work mirrors aspects of the evolutionary path of modern design along the central lines documented by Pevsner, it also reflects another equally significant aspect of late nineteenth-century design, yet one that is often

relegated to the footnotes of history. The cult of the exotic was a strong element of late nineteenth-century taste and one that was fed by a great many painters, decorators and craftsmen. The retail and decorating firm of Liberty's advertised 'Eastern Art Manufactures from Persia, India, China and Japan'. Louis Comfort Tiffany in New York founded a decorating company in 1879 that promoted a highly wrought neo-Byzantine style incorporating mosaics and elaborate metalwork, before turning his energies to the re-creation of the magical lustres and surface effects of ancient Middle-Eastern glassware. In France, from the time of the Romantics, from the time of Gustave Flaubert's tour in 1849–51 with the photographer Maxime du Camp to record the magical ruins of ancient Middle-Eastern cultures, images of an idealised version of the land of *A Thousand and One Nights* had known great popularity. Orientalist painters were in vogue, though their harems and Salaambos tell us more about the French than the Arabs. In England the vogue was for a romanticised vision of ancient Rome, as rendered with cinematic verisimilitude by Sir Lawrence Alma Tadema or, with a lighter, more romantic touch, by Albert Moore. But this vision of Rome was a reflection on the mores of London's St John's Wood rather than those of the ancient city and its people. What is so relevant about each of these examples is less the specific aspect of real history chosen as the starting point of inspiration than the collective need for some kind of escapist exotica. Simon Jervis, in his study of Carlo's furniture, lists some of the modish terms used to describe the fashionable interiors of the 1870s and 1880s – 'Moresque', 'Alhambra', 'Cairene', 'Turkish' and 'Arabian' – but, because Carlo's furniture does not borrow specific details from Middle-Eastern styles, he seems reluctant to accept that it is truly part of the contemporary cult. The decorative references, however, did not need to be specific for the furniture to satisfy the demand for a flavour of the exotic, and it in no way detracts from Carlo's originality to suggest that he was indeed very much a part of this fashion. A critic wrote in 1888 in *The Journal of Decorative Art* that Carlo's furniture would 'delight the heart of Alma Tadema'.

A chronological study of Carlo Bugatti's furniture designs would logically subdivide them into three more or less distinct modes. The first could be aptly described by

*An extraordinary bench seat, designed en suite with the vitrine and table illustrated on page 16. Another version of this fringed and tasselled piece of exotica is in the collection of the Metropolitan Museum of Art, New York.*

the contemporary epithet 'quaint'; the second, during the 1890s, displays a more individual boldness, with a greater use of vellum and a reliance on the circle or part circle as the basis of structural design; the third and consummate phase, exemplified by the 1902 Turin exhibit, is characterised by schemes of an extraordinary sculptural, serpentine freedom.

The earliest known example of Carlo's furniture is the bedroom suite made to celebrate the marriage of his sister to Segantini in 1880. A close scrutiny of this ensemble will help to identify the characteristics of the first design phase. The basic structure is of dark wood. The forms, notably of the pair of chairs and the head and foot boards of the bed itself, tend to a heaviness that is hardly relieved by the choice of wood. The spindly turned wood uprights and the inventive asymmetric substructure of the bedside cabinet introduce the only elements of lightness. The wrappings and applications of wrought copper, the galleries and fretted details provide a strong pseudo-Arab element, while the still naturalistic painted decoration acknowledges the taste for *Japonaiserie*. Discreet inlaid friezes and applied strips of pale wood and ivory complete the decoration.

A similar character pervades the next datable group of furniture designs, the exhibit prepared by Carlo for the 1888 Italian Exhibition at Earl's Court, London, and documented in some detail in contemporary periodicals. *The Queen, The Lady's Newspaper* of 7 July 1888 describes and illustrates nine examples of 'Quaint Furniture Exhibited by Carlo Bugatti, Milan'. The writer appealed to 'Lovers of decorative furniture, artistic in design and execution, quaint and novel in arrangement, and quite exceptional in effect' to 'closely study the exhibits of Signor Carlo Bugatti of Milan', and proceeded to describe in detail some of the most striking specimens. First was a chair of ebonised wood, described significantly as 'inlaid in white metal in Mauresque style'. An occasional table fringed with silk and leather has, like the above-mentioned chair, chamois leather panels with naturalistic painted decoration. Another chair is described, again significantly, as having 'a Japanese floral design' painted in brown and gold. A footstool upholstered in chamois has a painted decoration, also 'in Mauresque style'. The epithets seem curiously interchangeable. A mirror arrangement, fringed and heavily decorated with repoussé metal, is described as

*An asymmetric wall bracket, a good example of Carlo's pseudo-arabic style, dating probably from about 1890. It is similar to one of Carlo's exhibits at the 1888 Italian Exhibition at Earl's Court, London, illustrated overleaf.*

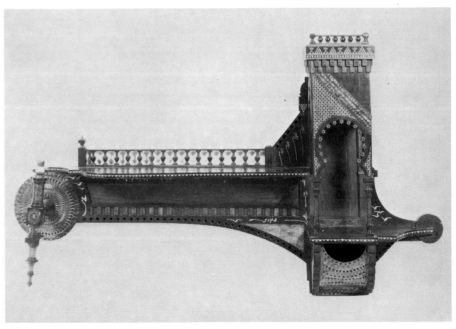

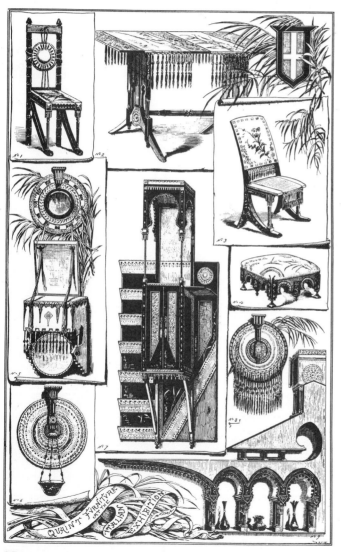

being decorated 'in Arabian style'. A curious wall bracket *étagère*, described as a 'most quaint construction', is of white wood inlaid with ebony, ivory, mother-of-pearl and white metal. The asymmetric design centres around a series of pseudo-Arab arches. A noticeable feature of the metal inlays is the repeated use of motifs that resemble a stylised script, neither arabic nor oriental yet evocative of both. *The Journal of Decorative Art* illustrated a remarkable exhibit, a screen that was a hotch-potch of all the ingredients of Carlo's early style, its repoussé metalwork including shields and elaborate hinges, abstract 'script' inlaid in metal into ebony, ivory details, asymmetric painted plant motifs and a curious elaborately framed mirror set, as if at random, on one side. The whole exhibit won Carlo a Diploma of Honour, awarded for the originality of his designs.

By the mid-1890s a second phase was in evidence. Its most obvious characteristics were the increasing use of vellum, frequently undecorated, or at most bearing slender plant sprays painted in brown with a light and elegant touch, a new boldness of form and the beginnings of Carlo's increasing passion for geometrically disciplined pattern making. From this period date two complete suites that have turned up in recent years at Sotheby's, the first in London on 5 July 1974, the second in Zurich on 6 May 1975; a bedroom suite, and certain pieces in the Metropolitan Museum of Art in New York, notably a fall-front desk. The natural beauty of the light sand-coloured vellum is intelligently exploited, providing a pleasing neutral foil to the elaborate inlaid borders or repoussé metalwork. The vellum, however, although playing an increasingly important role, is not allowed to disguise the essential wooden framework of the furniture it adorns. Designs from this period are obsessively dominated by the circle or part circle. The desk in the Metropolitan Museum has a circular front falling from a central cylindrical cabinet within an elaborate rectangular frame. A cabinet in the Sotheby London sale has a central circle offset within another; the crescent-shaped diminishing margin between the two circles contains a meticulously drawn and inlaid, similarly diminishing, repeat motif. The geometric inlays of this period, in white and yellow metals and pale wood and ebony, are totally abstract yet have the character of highly formalised insects. Two facts bear witness to Carlo's increasing success at this time: first the fact that his

*A decorative screen, designed en suite with the furniture shown on pages 16 and 20. The detail (left) demonstrates the intricacy of Carlo's designs at this period. The insect-like inlay is a favorite theme which occurs in his furniture, drawings, silver and jewellery designs.*

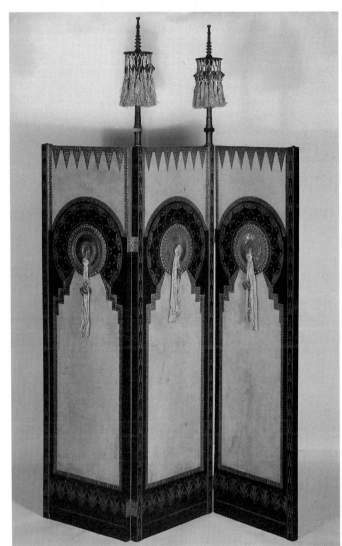

designs were being pirated by at least one firm, Ernest Kopp & Co of Berlin; second that the decade was crowned by the Silver Medal awarded at the Paris Exposition Universelle of 1900. Around 1900 the Mussulman architect Antoine Losciac commissioned furniture from Carlo for the Constantinople residence of the Khedive's mother – a curious confirmation of the appeal of the artist's originality.

Carlo's third, final and most interesting mode of design burst forth to a surprised and sometimes bewildered public at Turin's first International Exhibition of the Decorative Arts in 1902. Here, on his native soil, Carlo Bugatti presented four rooms as well as a group of individual items of furniture. The interiors were complete and uncompromising, with wall panelling and specially woven carpets giving an organic completeness to the schemes. Vellum now reigned supreme, completely covering the wooden structure of the furnishings, neatly disguising joints and creating an illusion of furniture moulded in a plastic medium. In the reception room the sweeping lines of banquettes remind one of the spirited freedom of Gaudi's outdoor seating in the Park Guell; a circular table-top sits on a curiously alive, tightly coiled base. The shapes of individual pieces are quite without precedent and truly extraordinary. Carlo introduces his novel chairs, conceived in one single sweeping line. Circles, part circles and ovoids create endless patterns; a rectangular cabinet is swallowed up within its dynamic sweeping frame. The elegant stylised patterns, insect forms or the pure geometry of Carlo's formerly inlaid decorations, are now painted with confidence and refinement directly onto the vellum in gold and pastel shades. Despite the apparent bewilderment of the judges, their decision was unanimous – to award the Diploma of Honour to Carlo Bugatti for this final flowering of his bizarre genius as a decorator and furniture designer.

The earliest mentions of the last phase of Carlo's career, his silverware, appear in the context of his exhibit in 1907 at the gallery of A. A. Hébrard, best known as a founder of art bronzes, including those of Carlo's son Rembrandt. Hébrard had a show-room on the smart rue Royale in Paris and he exhibited, with great discrimination, the work of leading craftsmen and artists. The Hébrard label has come to be regarded as a measure of quality. The exhibition ran from 2 to 25 December and it was here that the correspondent of *The Studio* was attracted by '. . . a

*Below: not all Carlo's designs relied on bizarre forms and complex decoration, but his originality of thought is still apparent in this bicycle, one of his many other design projects.*

*Opposite: this glass-seated chair, a companion to the one illustrated overleaf, is typical of the second phase of Carlo's furniture, in which pure geometry and lightly decorated vellum play an increasingly important part. The cabinet contains more elements of Carlo's earlier 'arabic' style, but combines these with the familiar insect inlay.*

*This armchair is a final example of the suite of furniture, including the cabinet on page 19 and the chair on page 25, designed by Carlo in the late 1890s.*

beautiful silver dish, with fishes as the decorative motifs'. He continued, however, with the comments that 'this artist, in striving to give proof of imaginativeness, has fallen into strange extravagances. I should not care for a service of which the *cafetière*, the sugar basin and milk-ewer took the shape of an elephant's head adorned with huge ivory tusks!' The description could almost be that of the silver service that appeared in a sale at Sotheby's Belgravia on 8 December 1978, though closer inspection of this reveals not a series of elephants but an assortment of vividly conceived creatures, figments of an extraordinary imagination but borrowing, haphazardly, elements from identifiable animals. L'Ebé tells us that her grandfather christened such creations '*Ses Bêtes*' – *his* creatures – not satisfied merely to stylise existing animals, but preferring to take the parts of them that he deemed beautiful and to combine them to create a menagerie both picturesque and novel. Hébrard provided the facilities and craftsmen to cast and chase the silver to Carlo's designs, acting both as manufacturer and retailer. It would seem that he was also a personal patron of Carlo's work, for a silver service by him illustrated in *Art et Décoration* is described as being from the collection of A. A. Hébrard. A better collaborator could hardly have been found, for the quality of execution of the silverware is of the high standard needed to convey the detailed and precise perfection of Carlo's designs. No better example could be called upon than the magnificent teapot sold at Sotheby's Belgravia on 8 December 1978. Here is a marvellous contrast of an organic free-form base, finely chased and incorporating naturalistic grotesques, surmounted by a body, spout and handle designed around the highly stylised bodies, legs and wings of insects and rendered with the crisp confidence of a piece of fine engineering. The hinged cover, on opening, clears the handle by a hair's breadth.

After the exhibition chez Hébrard, we are kept aware of Carlo's continuing interest in silver through the accounts of his exhibits at the annual Salon de la Société des Artistes Décorateurs. In 1910, at the fifth Salon, a commentator in *Art et Décoration* drew attention to a tea and coffee service in cast and hammered silver on the theme of the dragonfly, an insect dear to Carlo since he first painted it, in highly stylised form, on his vellum furniture. The following year another service on the dragonfly theme elicited a mixture of praise and criticism in the pages of the same magazine.

A table/cabinet in wood covered in painted vellum with applied motifs in metal, designed by Carlo in the final phase of his furniture design. The vellum disguises joints, giving the illusion that the furniture is moulded rather than built up.

An elegant chair, in wood and vellum, from a dining suite created by Carlo for his own use quite late in his career. Its dependence on a continuous sweeping line shows a debt to the ideas of the Art Nouveau movement.

*One of the four rooms presented by Carlo at the Turin Exhibition of 1902. The sweeping shapes are quite without precedent, though earlier decorative features still persist.*

The author wrote that the service 'paid homage to M Carlo Bugatti's ingenuity', but he added 'Is this however an example of logically designed silver for everyday use and of easy upkeep?' The answer was in the negative. A bizarre feature of the service in question, and indeed of other examples of Carlo's silver, was his grotesque menagerie's appetite for their own and other creatures' tails. It seems somehow irrelevant to discuss or criticise such work in terms of functionalistic ideals.

During this later phase of his career, in which he turned his attention to smaller-scale works, Carlo produced a series of designs for jewellery. A surviving sketchbook contains, in addition to working sketches for a silver tea service similar to that sold at Sotheby's, designs for two items of jewellery on the theme of the dragonfly – a hair comb and a pendant – and a revealing series of sketches of dragonflies in varying degrees of stylisation. L'Ebé describes a *parure* made for her mother in turquoise and brilliants comprising a necklace, ear-rings, and a ring and bracelet linked by ornamental chains over the back of the hand. The decorative motif, repeated in each piece, was the scarab. Carlo's interest in female ornament was not limited to jewellery design, and L'Ebé records his creation in about 1903 of *parures* in repoussé suede.

Among other flowerings of Carlo's diverse talents was his creation of a series of stringed musical instruments on the principle of the guitar, but of a form and concept entirely without precedent. One such was a 30-stringed creation, nearly one and a half metres high and three quarters of a metre wide, decorated in the characteristic painted vellum. This was played by Carlo's wife and a certain Maitre Moceri. Other minor eccentricities detailed by L'Ebé include a leather wallet without seams and a single-wheeled racing buggy!

A diverse and at times bewildering talent, Carlo Bugatti nimbly defies easy categorisation. In an age of contradictions there are opposite elements even within this one artist's work. Creations of a seemingly baroque elaboration reveal, on closer inspection, elements of pure logic, and the whimsical decorator is revealed as a disciplined and, at times, visionary designer. To take one example, his G-shaped chairs for the 'Snail' room at the Turin Exhibition, the design of which was so novel as to meet with misunderstanding and mockery, had nevertheless a twofold importance. Here was a highly

The 'Snail' room from the Turin Exhibition, with its G-shaped chairs, shows the fluidity, sculptural freedom and inventiveness of this final phase of Carlo's furniture designs to even greater effect. It was not to be surpassed. With this exhibit, Carlo had played his ace and he was soon to abandon his interest in furniture design in favour of smaller-scale works.

intelligent solution to the problem of seat design, allowing space behind the circular seat for the overhang of coat tails or train; here also in its freedom of form was a precursor of what was to become, some 50 years later, a commercially viable proposition with the introduction of glass fibre and injection-moulded plastics.

Carlo's passion for decoration was perhaps the essence of his talent. During his most sophisticated period, from about the mid-1890s on, he displayed brilliance as a graphic artist and his furniture and silver are worthy of study in close-up, the detail being often more fascinating and revealing than the whole. Seduced, like so many of his contemporaries, by the romance of the exotic, Carlo nevertheless succeeded in giving a personal twist to this fashion, making it an integral and attractive part of his work. Preserving, and indeed cultivating, his individuality, helping to shape, as well as being shaped by, the era in which he lived, he emerges as a single-minded, highly individualistic talent to whom there was no possibility of compromise.

## BIOGRAPHICAL SUMMARY

| | |
|---|---|
| 1856 | Born Milan 12 February |
| 1880 | Married Thérèse Lorioli |
| | Created bedroom suite for sister and brother-in-law Segantini |
| 1888 | Established workshop at 6 Via Castelfidardo, Milan. Diploma of Honour at Italian Exhibition, London |
| 1900 | Silver Medal at Exposition Universelle, Paris |
| 1902 | Diploma of Honour at Turin Exhibition |
| 1904 | Moved to Paris |
| 1907 | Exhibition of silverware at Galerie Hébrard 2 to 25 December |
| c1910 | Moved to Pierrefonds |
| 1935 | Death of wife |
| c1937 | Moved to Molsheim |
| 1940 | Died April at Château St Jean, Dorlisheim, Bas-Rhin |

BIBLIOGRAPHY

Carlo Bugatti's work is mentioned in many journals of the period, including *The Journal of Decorative Art; The Cabinet Maker and Art Furnisher; The Queen, The Lady's Newspaper; Deutsche Kunst und Dekoration; Kunst und Kunsthandwerk; Art et Décoration*; and *The Studio*. More extensive references are given below.

Rossi-Sacchetti, V. *Rembrandt Bugatti, Sculpteur. Carlo Bugatti et son Art*. Paris, Imprimerie de Vaugirard, 1907 (illustrated with portraits)

Spadini, Pasqualina, and Maino, Maria Paolo. *Carlo Bugatti. I Mobili Scultura*. Rome, Galleria dell'Emporio Floreale, 1976 (illustrated catalogue of work by Carlo, Rembrandt and Ettore)

Bugatti, L'Ebé. *Unpublished notes on Carlo Bugatti* (19pp typescript)

Jervis, Simon. 'Carlo Bugatti' in *Arte Illustra* no. 3, 1970, pp34–36, pp80–87

Bugatti, L'Ebé. *The Bugatti Story*. London, 1967

Pica, Vittore. *L'Arte Decorativa all'Esposizione di Torino*. Bergamo, 1902

*L'Ebé Bugatti, painted in oils as a young woman by her grandfather Carlo.*

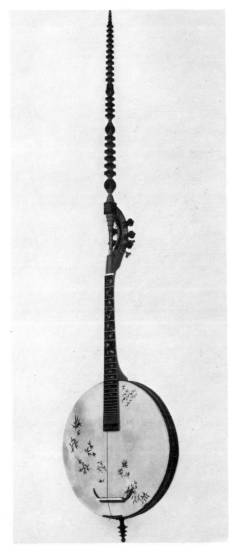

*A stringed instrument in inlaid wood and painted vellum that is typical of Carlo's eccentric exercises in the field.*

*Above: the years that Rembrandt Bugatti spent at Antwerp Zoo were the happiest and most prolific of his life. The Zoo welcomed and fostered artists, and most of Rembrandt's most famous sculptures were modelled there. Long after his tragic early death, his memory was kept alive by the Zoo's prize for animal sculpture, and the major retrospective exhibition organised in 1955 at the Zoo began the modern revival of interest in his work.*

*Left: all Rembrandt's bronzes were signed, usually 'R. Bugatti', as illustrated here. The majority were cast by the famous Hébrard foundry in Paris by the lost wax process and bear the stamp 'Cire Perdue – A. A. Hébrard' as well as the cast number.*

# Rembrandt Bugatti 1885-1916

Mary Harvey

When the extraordinary Bugatti family's talent for original expression reached Carlo's younger son Rembrandt, it was distilled into some of the greatest animal sculptures of modern times. Like his father's furniture and his brother's automobiles, Rembrandt's sculptures are immediately recognisable and distinguishable from any other work; his mastery of petrifying the single gesture that characterises his model has never been equalled, before or since.

Unlike so many artists, he achieved recognition and acclaim at an early age and, although his life was so short, tragically ended by his suicide at 30, he made a deep impression on the art world during his brief working life between 1901 and 1916. There are very few artists who could claim such immediate success as his, and fewer still who received such financial reward in their early 20s. The Paris Salons exhibited his work each year, articles and books were published about him, museums acquired his work, and he was made a Chevalier of the Legion of Honour at the age of 26. This very formidable reputation died with him, to an extent, and until recently the name Bugatti meant cars to most people, only a few associating it also with beautiful sculpture. So who was this mysterious and tragic 'other Bugatti'?

Born in Milan on 16 October 1885, Rembrandt was always aware that his elder brother Ettore was their mother's favourite, she being apparently unable to forgive Rembrandt for his difficult birth and the subsequent long illness she suffered. Throughout his life Rembrandt was shy and solitary, with very few close friends or female companions, but all who knew him have testified to his gentleness and kindness. In sympathetic company he was a very good conversationalist with a fine sense of humour and capable of moments of great gaiety, but the melancholy that always hung about him deepened as he grew older into depression and eventual suicide.

As a child Rembrandt lived in the shadow of his exuberant, extrovert brother, but they were very devoted and always took a great interest in each other's achievements. The two boys and their sister Deanice were fortunate to be brought up in an affluent, slightly bohemian, middle-class home by parents who were very social. Their father Carlo attracted a wide circle of friends through his many interests, and the family home, first in Milan and then in Paris, was a lively meeting-place where visitors might include the composers Leoncavallo, Puccini and his librettist Illica, Ricordi the music publisher, the sculptor Ercole Rosa (who was Rembrandt's godfather and who gave him his prophetic christian name), and artists Arturo Rietti and Segantini, as well as many distinguished critics and writers, notably Leon Tolstoy.

Carlo Bugatti brought his sons up to work and made them spend many hours in his studio, helping him to produce elaborate metal ornamentation for his furniture. Although possibly unrewarding at the time, this apprenticeship developed in the boys the great manual skill and ability to work with metals that they both drew on to such good effect later.

It was decided that Ettore should become an artist and he was sent to study painting and architecture at the Brera Academy of Fine Arts in Milan. Rembrandt, who as a young teenager was a complete enigma to his family and schoolteachers, was thought to be destined for a career in engineering. However, his true talent came to light in a very dramatic way one day when his father was entertaining a friend in his studio. While looking at new works, the visitor lifted a damp cloth to reveal a very accomplished clay group of three cows led by a peasant. Denying any knowledge of this work, Carlo was astounded to discover that the true author was Rembrandt, then aged 15, but he readily accepted that he had been wrong and that his younger son must make a career in art; from then on he gave him every encouragement to do so. At about the same time, Ettore realised that he would never have anything like his brother's artistic talent and switched to engineering – a success story that is recorded elsewhere in this book.

Unlike his brother, Rembrandt had no formal art school training and can be said to be entirely self taught, but the completeness of his early work is very impressive. The 'Cow' dated 1901 must be one of his earliest cast works, probably modelled at about the same time as the group mentioned above, and if one compares it with sculptures he made a decade later, one can see that the style has hardly altered and that there is no sign of immaturity in the earlier piece, cast when the artist was only 16.

Possibly the only outside influence on him at that time came from Prince Paul Troubetzkoy, who was a frequent visitor to the Bugatti family home. A Russian aristocrat, born in Italy, who had reached the height of fame in Paris as a portrait sculptor, Troubetzkoy was an international success who sculpted many famous figures of the time, including Tolstoy, Puccini and Tsar Alexander III. Above all he is known for his very beautiful sculptures of women – society ladies with their dogs, ballerinas, actresses and so on. It has often been said that he taught Rembrandt to sculpt, but this would seem to be an overstatement. What

he certainly did do was to stimulate the interest of this timid, rather strange boy by allowing him to come to his studio to observe, and he persuaded him to begin modelling clay with his fingers, instead of carving wood as he had done in his father's studio. Rembrandt would also have been fascinated by Troubetzkoy's sculptures of animals, his own preoccupation. Troubetzkoy, who had himself been much influenced by Rodin, encouraged Rembrandt to develop a very free style that depended on working at some speed to achieve a total impression rather than concentrating on detail. This must have confirmed the very strong urge that the boy already had to work in this way.

In 1903 two of Rembrandt's sculptures were accepted for exhibition in the Venice Biennale d'Arte. The catalogue lists them simply as 'Horses' and 'Dog', so we cannot be sure what they were, but it is possible that the former model was the 'Horsefair' mentioned later.

In 1904 the family moved to Paris, where Carlo had increasingly established his reputation and his career. Rembrandt, then 19, spent most of his time at the Jardins des Plantes, studying, drawing and modelling the great

*Left: 'Cow', dated in Rembrandt's writing '01'. So far the earliest recorded bronze by Rembrandt, cast when he was only 16. 23 × 38cm.*

*Opposite: 'Ten Minutes' Rest', dated 1905 and inscribed 'Pièce Unique'. Also known as 'Le Grand Fardier', the wax of this impressive group of dray horses pausing to feed was exhibited at the Salon Nationale in 1905. The sculpture won the Grand Prix in the Milan Exhibition of 1906. It is shown in Ettore Bugatti's home. 255 × 38 × 50cm.*

variety of animals in that historic zoo. In the same year he exhibited four plaster models in the Salon of the Société Nationale des Beaux-Arts, one of which was the group of 'Two Stags'. His work attracted the attention of Adrien Hébrard, owner of the newspaper *Le Temps* and of the Galerie Hébrard at 8 rue Royale. Carlo had already undertaken several commissions for this colourful entrepreneur, who lost no time in putting his son under contract. Hébrard owned a foundry that cast the work of his artists, a stable that included Dalou, Degas, Pompon and Troubetzkoy. Bronzes cast by the foundry were of the highest quality, renowned for their rich dark patina, and although in future years Rembrandt came to resent the ties that bound him to Hébrard, feeling that the latter had exploited him, there is no doubt that he could not have had a finer start than under this patron. Every year a major exhibition of his work was held at the Galerie Hébrard, and these shows, together with the work exhibited at the annual salons, established his reputation and brought him great rewards, both financial and in prestige. Hébrard was a very great showman and probably drew the public's and critics' attention to this very self-effacing young man much

earlier than would have been the case had he tried to succeed on his own.

In the first exhibition at Galerie Hébrard, held in 1904, some 30 plaster models were shown, including the famous 'Horsefair'. This subject was eventually cast as a bronze measuring 2.7 metres in length. It was inscribed 'Pièce Unique', one bronze only being cast from it. Before this, however, the plaster had undergone many alterations, several of the individual horses being swapped around or even replaced until Rembrandt was satisfied that he had achieved the right composition. It is, in fact, an extremely daring arrangement and one that succeeds brilliantly. For many years the bronze took pride of place at Ettore's house at Molsheim, and it can be seen in the window in several photographs taken of it during the 1920s and 1930s. It has been included in most major exhibitions of Rembrandt's work and is now one of the most important items in a private collection in England.

Rembrandt Bugatti broke the tradition of portraying a single animal in a sculpture, an earlier exception to this general rule having been the familiar groups by the nineteenth-century *Animalier* sculptors of carnivores

A charming early example of Rembrandt's liking for compositions that included different animals of contrasting size, shape or texture, this group of 'Elephant and Young Camel' was exhibited at the Salon Nationale in 1905. 46cm long.

Left: 'Three Cassowaries', a fine group showing the birds in different poses, each typical of the species. At least one of them has also been cast separately.

Opposite: 'The Horsefair', the first of Rembrandt's three large horse groups, each a unique cast. This portrait of two old peasants taking their horses to sell at a fair is probably the best known. It was exhibited at the Salon Nationale in 1905 and in the retrospective exhibition of Rembrandt's work at the Salon d'Automne in 1973. 270 × 68 × 50cm.

seizing and devouring their prey – a violent theme that Rembrandt would have hated. He liked to create groups of animals, emphasising the differences between them; the 'Elephant and Young Camel', which was exhibited at the Salon Nationale in 1905, is a charming early example of this sort of composition. Sometimes a large group would be split, with each animal cast as a separate bronze, but far from removing the meaning of the piece, it could then be seen that each animal was a complete work in itself, observed and portrayed on its own, but when put together in one group each animal interacted harmoniously with the rest. The 'Three Cassowaries' have sometimes been cast separately, as have the 'Leopards'.

The first exhibition at the Galerie Hébrard had excellent reviews, all the critics commenting on the innovative quality of Rembrandt's work. A typical example appeared in *Art Décoratif* (Vol2, p41, 1904) whose critic, having stated that he found Bugatti's sculptures to be completely original and that they did not bring to mind the work of any previous animal sculptor, went on to say: 'The truth is that M Bugatti scrupulously portrays his models in attitudes that are the most natural and at the same time the least often translated into sculpture, and if he preserves in his works the quality of sketches, it is certainly less for reasons of *ambiance* and light than for fear of destroying by overwork the honesty and sensitivity that are, as has been said, the characteristic qualities of this newcomer.' (*Author's translation*).

The exhibition of Rembrandt's new work became an annual feature at the Galerie Hébrard until his death, after which in 1920 Hébrard staged a major retrospective in his memory, including 125 works. Rembrandt also exhibited his new work every year at the Salon of the Société Nationale des Beaux-Arts, and in most years at the Salon d'Automne, as well as at the Venice Biennale d'Arte.

In 1907 Rembrandt made the most important change in his life by going to live in Antwerp, where he remained until a year or so before he died. He made short trips to Italy and Paris for exhibitions, and to Molsheim where his brother Ettore had established his home and his factory, but he was always glad to get back to Antwerp where he felt at home in the congenial and bohemian company of the artists' colony in which he lived. His move to this provincial Belgian town was, in fact, very logical. It had

*Although Rembrandt's main interest was in sculpting animals, he created several masterly portraits of people, such as this very striking model of 'The Appleseller', a peasant woman who stood at the gates of Antwerp Zoo every day and was his great friend. This sculpture was exhibited at the Salon Nationale in 1913. 66 × 36 × 36cm.*

been an artistic centre since the Middle Ages, but its greatest attraction for Rembrandt were its zoological gardens, managed by the Royal Zoological Society of Antwerp, which were right in the centre of town, next to the railway station. These were so short of space that animal enclosures had to be designed in terraces, one above another, but they were rich in subjects for his sculpture. The Antwerp Zoo has always had one of the greatest and most diverse collections of animals in the world, and in the early part of the present century it had the pick of rare species from the Belgian colonies in Africa and Asia. Rembrandt was fascinated by this wealth of beautiful and curious animals, and depicted many species that more orthodox sculptors would have spurned, such as vultures, ant-eaters, snakes and so on.

Antwerp Zoo encouraged artists, even offering them a studio in the grounds in which to work, and they were allowed complete freedom to set up easels and all their other paraphernalia wherever they wished. Regular exhibitions of work by resident artists were held by the zoo, and these sold well to the local affluent and appreciative middle class. (Unfortunately much of the bronze sculpture acquired by Antwerp citizens, probably including work by Rembrandt, is presumed to have been destroyed during the Second World War when a great amount of metalwork was taken by the occupying German forces to be melted down for munitions.) A close circle of animal painters and sculptors was attracted by this stimulating environment and produced diverse work of a very high quality. Over the years the zoo authorities astutely acquired examples of the work of quite a few of these artists and their Museum now has a most interesting and valuable collection, which must be visited by anyone interested in animal art. Rembrandt's contemporaries are well represented; the artists whose work most nearly approaches his being Alberic Collin (1886–1962), who shared his studio apartment and was a constant companion. The recent revival of the public's interest in animal sculpture has led to a new appreciation of Collin's beautifully observed small mammals and birds and, as well as six small bronzes in the Museum, there are two life-size statues of a cheetah and of a leopard in the grounds of the zoo. Other sculptors with whom Rembrandt mixed daily and who have since achieved importance are Arthur Dupon, Eduard Deckers, Oscar Jespers, Frans Jochems

*'Great Indian Rhinoceros', a beautiful study which conveys perfectly the bulk and strength of this intractable animal, modelled about 1906. 43 × 62cm.*

*'Brown Bear', a later model, circa 1912. Plasters of this work are in the National Gallery of Modern Art, Rome, and the Musée de Louvre, Paris. 40 × 50cm.*

and Josué Dupon, who created many large animal groups including the monumental statue of a camel and its driver that stands on the roof of the zoo's main building and is a landmark of the city. Paul Jouve, who is probably best known for his illustrations of Kipling's *Jungle Book*, and the painter and engraver Walter Vaes were also among Rembrandt's colleagues. The zoo's museum includes a special gift of nearly 30 sculptures by Jaap Kaas (born 1898), who became Professor of Sculpture and Drawing at Rotterdam Academy and was a child when Rembrandt was working at the zoo, but was fascinated by the animals and made his first studies there at that time.

The general atmosphere suited Rembrandt and this was the most prolific period of his life, the majority of his sculptures being produced during his seven years at Antwerp. His output was quite astonishing, particularly in view of the fact that he destroyed many more models in the early stages than were ever cast in bronze. A total of nearly 200 completed models has been recorded.

His tools had been made specially to his design at Ettore's Molsheim factory, and were used for finishing work, but the actual modelling was always done with his hands and his fingerprints can be seen quite clearly in the finished bronzes, adding to the impression of a fleeting moment captured which is such a characteristic of Rembrandt's work.

He had an instinctive grasp of shape and form that made the taking of measurements unnecessary and this, coupled with the manual dexterity he had developed at an early age, enabled him to work very quickly. He set out to capture a certain pose rather than anatomical perfection, but in the end his general competence realised both.

He would spend a long time studying a subject, perhaps as much as two hours, before beginning work, and then he seemed to be suddenly possessed with a feverish impulse. Having constructed a wire basis, or armature, he rapidly filled in the shape of the animal, forming the clay in his fingers. Occasionally he had more than one model going at the same time and would move back and forth between them, but any study that was incomplete by the end of a session was abandoned; no models were ever returned to and worked on at a later date. In his studio at night he would carefully examine the day's work to decide what to discard and what to finish off and send to Hébrard to be cast.

The finished clay model would be cast as a plaster in the first instance, and then as a bronze by the lost wax or *cire perdue* process – a skilful and elaborate operation which is too complicated to explain in great detail here, but since the excellence of the Hébrard casts make a considerable contribution to the beauty of Rembrandt's bronzes, it may be of interest to describe briefly how they were created. The same basic method is in use today, although more sophisticated aids are now available.

By using what is known as a 'waste mould', a plaster replica is cast from the original clay model. This plaster cast is then used to make a negative rubber mould (gelatine would have been used in Rembrandt's day) which is in two or more pieces according to the complexity of the work and has an outer casing of plaster to strengthen it. Liquid wax is then poured into this mould and, as it cools, the liquid core is tipped out, leaving a hollow wax shell. The plaster casing is removed and the rubber mould peeled from the wax; at this stage the artist may work on the wax to sharpen the detail or even make some slight alteration. At several of the Salon exhibitions Rembrandt showed his work at the wax stage, which was quite legitimate since the waxes would have been perfect replicas of his original clay models.

A strengthened plaster mould is then made around the wax, totally enveloping it and in one piece. Through a system of 'runners' the wax is melted out and the molten bronze is poured in – hence the title of the process. After the metal cools, the plaster mould is chipped off and discarded, but the emergent bronze still needs a lot of work done to it. This is known as 'chasing' and involves removing all the runners and replacing the detail where they touched the surface, as well as smoothing out any other faults. This after-work is usually supervised by the

*Top: 'French Bulldog' is one of Rembrandt's most popular models, this example is numbered 35. 14 × 14cm.*

*Right: casts of this well known 'Hamadryas Baboon' are in the Fine Arts Museum of San Francisco and the National Gallery of Modern Art, Rome. Around 1910 Rembrandt's work began to take on a more simplified style, possibly influenced by Cubism, clearly shown in this piece. 43 × 18 × 45cm.*

artist. Bronze is an alloy consisting mainly of copper with small amounts of tin, zinc and iron, and the colour of a 'raw' bronze sculpture is like that of a newly minted copper coin. The finished colour, or patina, is achieved by applying a variety of acids and alkalis that work on the surface to produce the colour specified by the artist, thus speeding up the natural process of oxidisation. Patinations can range through all the browns, from very pale to dark, a variety of antique greens can also be created, and bronzes are sometimes gilded or silvered. With a very few exceptions, Rembrandt chose the darkest patina possible for his bronzes, usually almost black, which was probably achieved by applying an ammonia solution with heat, and when polished this patination produces the soft rich glow that so enhances his work.

All Rembrandt's bronzes bear his signature, as well as the stamp of the foundry – 'Cire Perdue. A.A. Hébrard' – and a cast number. Unfortunately the Hébrard foundry no longer exists and its records are not available, so it is impossible to tell how many casts were made of each model. They were not made in a limited edition in the modern sense, when the number of bronzes to be cast is announced in advance, but they were, of course, limited in the sense that they were expensive and cast only to order. There were one or two small 'popular' models such as that of the French Bulldog, of which up to 40 bronzes are known to have been cast, but in the main it is rare to find any number higher than 10 on a Bugatti bronze.

Some of Rembrandt's bronzes are unique casts, such as the large 'Horsefair', which is inscribed by him 'Pièce Unique'. He does not seem to have had a standard practice of dating the bronzes, and only a few are inscribed with the year in which they were cast. The first, artist's proof does not have a number but bears the letter M, for *Modèle*. Some bronzes have a letter prefix to the number, such as A, but the reason for these separate series is not known at present. A very few of Rembrandt's bronzes were cast by the firm of Valsuani, another eminent Paris foundry, but so far as we know these did not have cast numbers.

Rembrandt loved animals deeply and had a great affinity with them. He detested any form of cruelty and, while he recognised that violence plays a part in all wild animals' lives, he never portrayed it in a sculpture. The nearest his work ever approached a carnivore devouring its prey were

his sculptures of big cats gnawing bones at the zoo. However, his intellect was sharp enough to protect him from the pitfall of sentimentalism, and although his animals are portrayed with tenderness and humour, there is no trace of anthropomorphism in any of his work.

Although his main preoccupation was with animals, he also made several masterly sculptures of human subjects, notably some very graceful statuettes of nude young women (his sensitivity was such that, the story goes, he requested one of his models to keep her lower half clothed because, he explained, he hated dirty feet). His portraits received very favourable comment, particularly for 'The Appleseller', a very strong figure of a peasant woman who stood at the gates of Antwerp Zoo and was an old friend of his. As a reaction to a criticism that he only made 'small drawing-room pieces' which were commercially popular, he borrowed the large studio of his friend Arthur Dupon and set to work to create a series of giant nude athletes modelled in clay, which he invited the critics to come and view *in situ*. His technical mastery was such that he found no difficulty in effecting this great change of scale. One, 'The Brute', was exhibited at the Salon des Artistes Italiens in Paris in 1907, and the author and critic V Rossi-Sacchetti wrote of it: 'Bent in a classic pose, the human animal is at rest, but at the same time ready to jump to his feet in revenge, hatred, cruelty and that destructive instinct that even the most refined civilisation will never be able to tame in the human soul . . . Bugatti demonstrates that "Man – the proud *Homo Sapiens*" has evolved from the same source as all the other animals of creation, and however much we may place ourselves on a superior level, the humble beings we have subjected to our tyranny have no reason to envy us. The human brute is there, crushing with its cruel and stubborn heaviness that pure gentleness, free from all guile, of creatures that it stupidly calls inferior.' (*Rembrandt Bugatti, Sculpteur. Carlo Bugatti et*

*Opposite: 'Walking Leopard', an early work which brilliantly captures the power and suppleness of the animal. 22 × 52cm.*

*Below: another early work, circa 1907, this beautifully observed group 'Pair of Courting Pelicans' forms a spectacular composition and demonstrates Rembrandt's original approach to design. 65 × 37 × 56cm.*

son *Art*. Paris Imprimerie de Vaugirard, 1907, p11. *Author's translation*.)

These monumental figures were later reproduced in stone, and one statue of a wrestler, one and a half times life-size, still stands menacingly on a hillside on a private estate in Provence.

Hébrard did not care for these monumental pieces at all and ignored them, but later Rembrandt created a series of small statuettes of male athletes for exhibition in the Galerie Hébrard. Around 1910 Rembrandt's work started to move towards a greater simplicity, developing into a style that was possibly influenced by Cubism. The 'Hamadryas Baboon', which dates from about 1910, shows the early stages of this style, while Rembrandt's last work, the 'Lioness and Serpent', shows the ultimate development in this direction and suggests even an Assyrian influence. This work was with the Valsuani foundry when Rembrandt died in 1916; it was cast posthumously and inscribed by Ettore.

Had Rembrandt lived the prescribed lifespan of 'three score years and ten' he would have died in 1960, and it is fascinating, though futile, to speculate how his work would have evolved from the 1920s onwards.

When the First World War began in August 1914, Rembrandt was 29 and his friends in Antwerp were concerned about his general well-being because he had become increasingly withdrawn and remote. The daughter of an artist friend, with whom Rembrandt had an 'understanding', turned him down and married someone else, and Rembrandt, who was shy with women generally, took this very badly. As the horror of the war unfolded, his depression deepened.

Although, as an Italian citizen, he could have obtained a safe pass to leave Belgium, he elected to stay and joined Antwerp Zoo's own Red Cross branch, which included several of his fellow artists. He and his friend Walter Vaes (who in happier days had made a portrait of Rembrandt) worked together tirelessly as stretcher-bearers and helped to look after the wounded who continually arrived at the makeshift hospital in the zoo's main hall. Rembrandt was emotionally quite unsuited to seeing such suffering, and zoo staff who worked with him during that time recalled later that, although he was a devoted nurse, he became quite overcome by the misery of it all. As the German

*Dated 1905, and possibly modelled from a family pet, this 'Pointer' has a companion piece which depicts a pointer bitch with puppies. Purists would detect the difference between this French breed and its British counterpart. 31 × 43cm.*

army advanced across Belgium his friends urged him to leave, and in November 1914 he arrived in Italy to join his brother in Milan for a while and then went to Paris.

He was now far from well, suffering from acute headaches and increasing deafness; in addition he had financial worries for the first time in his life, the art market being almost non-existent. He had no taste for work and only one or two pieces are recorded for this last year. The final blow came with the ending of a love affair that had blossomed briefly in 1915 – for Rembrandt the second rejection in two years. The combination of all his problems overcame him and he ended his life on 8 January 1916. He made elaborate, carefully planned preparations to do so, and witnesses who saw him alive on that day all testified to his calmness and even cheerfulness.

Early in the morning he went to Mass at the Madeleine and on leaving bought a bunch of violets from the flower-seller at the bottom of the steps of the church. He went back to the small studio in Montparnasse where he was then living, stopped up all the gaps around the doors and windows with newspapers, turned on the gas taps and then, elegantly dressed and wearing white gloves, he lay down on his bed to die. Although still just alive when found, he died on the way to hospital. He left two letters, which he had written to his brother and to the Superintendent of Police. Near his bedside was the bunch of violets placed next to his Legion of Honour Cross. His studio and his papers were in perfect order.

Ettore, who was devastated by his brother's death, arranged for him to be buried in the family vault at Dorlisheim and later gathered Rembrandt's sculptures together in a permanent exhibition at Molsheim. The family collection was later moved to the Château of Ermenonville in France, where Ettore's daughters continued to conserve it after his death in 1947.

Although retrospective exhibitions of Rembrandt's work were occasionally held after his death, notably at the Abdy Gallery in London, from which quite a few of the sculptures now in public collections were acquired, and at the Venice Biennale in 1932, generally his name was forgotten, except perhaps in Antwerp, where his loss was mourned by many friends and admirers. In 1947 the Royal Zoological Society of Antwerp founded the Bugatti Prize for Sculpture, 'in memory of the great *Animalier* sculptor

*Dated 1910 and inscribed in Rembrandt's writing 'Bison d'Amérique', this large bronze of a buffalo was exhibited at the Salon Nationale, Paris, in 1911. 41 × 74cm.*

who lived for several years in Antwerp and there created his most beautiful works at the Zoological Gardens'. The prize is awarded every other year to the most gifted pupil in the studio of animal sculpture at the Higher National Institute of Fine Arts at Antwerp. Through the persistence and enthusiasm of the zoo's Director, M Walter Van den bergh, a major retrospective exhibition was held at the Antwerp Zoo in 1955 which included many works belonging to the Bugatti family. It is no exaggeration to say that this exhibition was the start of Rembrandt's revival and did much to foster interest in his work among younger generations.

The decades between the two World Wars were years of great inconstancy of taste, when excellence was sometimes perhaps overlooked in the restless search for a new expression. Representational animal artists on the whole did not fare so well as those who adapted their subjects' shapes into stylised forms, or even into abstract patterns. In many of the schools of art that flourished briefly at this time, the animal did not figure at all.

Nothing is ever really new, and from the middle 1950s onwards the wheel began to turn full circle as an increasingly affluent, and therefore mobile, public visited zoos and the new safari parks and watched wildlife programmes on their newly acquired television sets. Animal books and magazines proliferated, and in the wake of all this renewed interest there followed a desire to own representations in painting and sculpture of animals as subjects in their own right. Many excellent contemporary artists helped to meet this demand, but the work of some of the earlier animal artists was also dusted down and reappraised.

The beauty of Rembrandt's animal sculptures was rediscovered and, for the second time this century, he was recognised as a genius. Throughout the 1960s exhibitions were held in many European capitals, and a major collection was included at the Salon d'Automne in Paris in 1973. Once again articles began to appear about him in art magazines. The steady rise in prices paid for his bronzes in the salerooms reflected this revival. It is possible that today's collectors are even more appreciative of his talents than the first owners, for his work has stood the test of time.

Rembrandt Bugatti's dazzling career was short, his debut and his departure equally dramatic, but he is now seen to have made a unique contribution to twentieth-century sculpture and to animal art in particular, and the 200 or so works that he created in 15 years endure as a permanent testament to this outstanding artist.

*Rembrandt's last work 'Lioness and Serpent' was at the foundry when he died. Cast posthumously, it was inscribed by his brother Ettore, 'Dernier oeuvre de mon frère, Paris 8 janvier 1916'. It shows the ultimate development of the more simplified style Rembrandt adopted in his later years, in which one can detect influences that are possibly Cubist, and perhaps even Assyrian. Ettore created a museum of his brother's work, first at Molsheim and then at Ermenonville, which his daughters continued to conserve after his death.*
*50 × 41 × 95cm.*

PUBLIC COLLECTIONS OWNING WORKS BY REMBRANDT
BUGATTI

*Belgium*
Musée des Beaux-Arts, Antwerp
Société Royale de Zoologie, Antwerp
Musées Royaux des Beaux-Arts, Brussels

*Czechoslovakia*
National Gallery, Prague

*East Germany*
National Gallery, East Berlin

*France*
Musée du Louvre, Paris
Direction des Beaux-Arts, Paris
Musée d'Art Moderne de la Ville de Paris
Musée d'Art Moderne, Strasbourg

*Great Britain*
Scottish National Gallery of Modern Art, Edinburgh
Tate Gallery, London

*Italy*
Galleria d'Arte Moderna, Brescia
Galleria Nazionale d'Arte Moderna, Rome
Museo d'Arte Moderna, Venice

*Sweden*
Nationalmuseum, Stockholm

*United States of America*
Cleveland Museum of Modern Art
Los Angeles County Museum of Art
Philadelphia Museum of Art
Fine Arts Gallery of San Diego
California Palace of the Legion of Honour, San Francisco

BIOGRAPHICAL SUMMARY

1885 Born Milan 16 October
1901 First known works cast in bronze
1903 First exhibited at Venice Biennale d'Arte
1904 Family moved to Paris
Exhibited four plasters at Salon of the Société
Nationale des Beaux-Arts, and elected a member
Signed contract with Adrien Hébrard
First exhibition at Galerie Hébrard
1907 Moved to Antwerp
1911 Elected Chevalier of the Legion of Honour
1914 At outbreak of war moved to Italy and then Paris
1916 Died 8 January

BIBLIOGRAPHY

Many articles about Rembrandt Bugatti have appeared in magazines, art journals and newspapers over the years, but they are too scattered to list here. A comprehensive bibliography, including all these published references, has been prepared by John R Kaiser of the Pennsylvania State University Libraries and can be found in *The Bronzes of Rembrandt Bugatti*, which is listed below along with the only other complete books that have been published about him.

Rossi-Sacchetti, V. *Rembrandt Bugatti, Sculpteur. Carlo Bugatti et son Art*. Paris, Imprimerie de Vaugirard, 1907 (illustrated with portraits)

Schlitz, Marcel. *Rembrandt Bugatti, 1885–1916*. Anvers, Société Royale de Zoologie, 1955 (illustrated with portraits, introduction by Richard Declerck)

Harvey, Mary. *The Bronzes of Rembrandt Bugatti. A Catalogue Raisonné*. London, Palaquin Publishing Ltd, 1979 (illustrated, with a bibliography by John R Kaiser)

Left: the young Ettore Bugatti in his workshop. Opposite: Ettore in about 1905, already with individual ideas on dress, like his father Carlo.

Below: the Molsheim team celebrates 'Le Patron's' fifty-first birthday. Ettore, his wife, his mother and father, and his children L'Ebé, Lidia, Jean and Roland are all there. So are the oldest employees, the major domo from the guesthouse, all the factory managers and the two senior designers, Bertrand and Nuss.

# Ettore Bugatti 1881-1947

Hugh Conway

Ettore Arco Isadoro Bugatti was born in 1881 into a home
in which the traditional skills of the artist and the mechanic
which dominated Milan society were much in evidence.
His father Carlo, if not a mechanic, was a superb craftsman
in wood and its decoration with metal, and no doubt could
have been a real mechanic if his interests had been so
inclined.

It was natural enough for Ettore to be encouraged to
follow in his father's artistic footsteps; he was sent to the
Art Academy at Brera to specialise in sculpture under
Prince Paul Troubetzkoy. Ettore himself has explained
what happened to change the course of his life – indeed,
much of what we know about him is derived from notes
that he dictated and left with his family, or gave to others
who were interested.

'My first ambition', he wrote, 'was to be a great artist,
and so earn the right to bear a name distinguished by my
father.

'My brother, who became the greatest Bugatti of our
line, had an eminent sculptor, Ercole Rosa, as a godfather.
He was born with a very large head, which made Rosa say
that he would become a great man or nothing at all; and in
order to help on his destiny Rosa advised giving him the
name Rembrandt.

'As the elder I had begun to study painting, sculpture
and architecture. I really tried very hard to be an artist in
the real sense of the word and not a builder in reinforced
concrete, who has a greater talent for handling
mathematics than producing shapes. I had the best
possible teachers in painting and sculpture, especially our
family friend, Prince Troubetzkoy, the quality of whose
works was well known.

'But then my brother suddenly took to drawing. I saw at
once, and confided in my dear mother, that he was the true
Bugatti and would soon be far better than I, in spite of my
studies, even if he were not already. I told her, too, that
two Bugattis in the same class might lead to confusion and

that under the circumstances I preferred to give up art.

'If a man has enough foresight to take such a decision he ought to thank God for it.

'Rembrandt wanted to be an engineer and build locomotives. I wanted to be an artist, but I was no more gifted for art than he was for mechanics. In fact, without any preparation or advice, he was already making good progress in the career which I had embarked upon.

'One day, some friends of my father asked me to try out a motor-tricycle which had been built a year after the appearance of the De Dion tricycle. It had been made by the firm of Prinetti and Stucchi. Prinetti was an engineer and Stucchi a very good industrialist, one of the best at that time, 1895.

'In a short while, just by looking at the machine, I had grasped all the intricacies of its mechanism. I should add that my father attached great importance to his two sons being able to work with their hands, and a cabinet-maker's work is the best of groundings for mechanics.

'Even in establishments of higher education, manual work would be of great value to those who are choosing a career, whatever that may be. It is a relaxation and at the same time exercises muscles and brain.

'I very quickly thought of modifications that could be made to the tricycle; some of them proved to be valid, and my ideas were nearly always considered by the engineers responsible for building it.

'I was taught how to use materials to the best advantage by a kindly man who saw everything very clearly, and his advice was the best teaching I could have had. He examined things keenly and judiciously, and his judgement was clear and unchallengeable. I often thought to myself that he was full of years and experience, and how happy I should be if I could ever know as much as he did . . .'
(From personal notes prepared by Ettore Bugatti and published by L'Ebé Bugatti in *L'Epopée Bugatti*, Paris 1966.)

The future course of his life was beginning to be set.

In 1897, at the age of 17, Ettore joined the cycle makers Prinetti and Stucchi as an apprentice. Soon he was being allowed to modify their machines and 'obtained authorisation to construct the first tricycle with two engines'. This is probably the machine that is illustrated in a line drawing in the *Automotor Journal*, October 1900, vol 5, p21

Ettore's interest in mechanically propelled vehicles extended beyond their design and construction into their competitive use. On 24 May 1899, at the age of 18, he entered his tricycle in the Paris-Bordeaux race, one of the early long-distance events in the new sport of automobile racing, but retired after hitting a dog and damaging the machine. There are records of him competing in several sprints or road races for tricycles in 1899, with wins and placings, in the many events run at that time in north Italy. Earning the reputation of a daredevil on the road, his urge now was to build a four-wheel car – a proper vehicle to compete with those appearing all over the world at this period of the birth of the motor vehicle.

The story has been told of how, unable to persuade Prinetti and Stucchi to produce the vehicle, he set about designing it at home. 'His own nature, cheerful and waggish, was little encouragement to others to take him seriously and associate themselves with him in a

*Above: Rembrandt designed a seal for his brother based on a young elephant balancing on a ball. Ettore later used it as a mascot for the Royale car.*

*Right: the 'Brindled Gnu' or 'Wildebeeste', dated 1907, is a superb example of Rembrandt's talent for capturing the essential characteristics of his subject. 34 × 43cm. The earlier group of 'Two Red Deer Stags', presumably modelled at the Jardins des Plantes, was included in the 1904 exhibition of the Salon Nationale, Paris, at which Rembrandt made his debut. 46 × 46cm.*

programme of construction. Then he started to make sketches of the multitude of ideas which crowded his brain. His father's studio was full of vast rolls of paper – Bugatti spent whole days designing the vehicle in pencil and crayon in all its detail.' (Author's translation from *Gazetta della Sport*, Milan, 10 May 1901.

Design was not enough; the vehicle must be built. Now Ettore was lucky: two friends of his father, the Counts Gulinelli of Ferrara, agreed to finance the project, with Carlo joining in to some measure. We are not clear exactly where the vehicle was constructed, but it was evidently not at Prinetti and Stucchi's premises. We read of the building of the car in 'Bugatti's workshop', and of the patterns and castings and small machined details, all of which could have been readily obtained in the Milan area.

The car first ran in the spring of 1901, its designer being then just 20 years old – an achievement that would be remarkable today, with all our knowledge of vehicle design, and astounding by any standards in 1901.

The car was a two seater, with a four-cylinder 90 × 120mm bore and stroke engine of three litres capacity, a four-speed gearbox and chain drive to the rear wheels. The inlet and exhaust valves were in the cylinder head, which was unusual if not novel at the time. It was shown at the International Exhibition at Milan in 1901 on the Ricordi stand, Cav J Ricordi being agent for several makes, alongside vehicles by Fiat, Isotta-Fraschini, Bianchi and de Dietrich. Contemporary comment referred to the car being the sensational novelty of the show, and indeed it was awarded the Milan City Cup for its design, after demonstration on the road.

Baron de Dietrich, from Niederbronn in Alsace, whose cars were on show at the exhibition alongside Ettore's, heard of his success and negotiated a licence to build the new car and for Bugatti to work for him as a consulting designer to produce cars to be called 'de Dietrich Bugatti'. A contract was signed by the two parties on 26 June 1902,

*Top: Ettore's first car, built in 1901 in Milan when he was 20.*

*Left: Ettore's early work for Baron de Dietrich was on large chassis. The car he is at the wheel of here was a 20hp model intended for racing in 1902.*

three months before Ettore's twenty-first birthday (Carlo was principal signatory to the document), and Ettore moved to Alsace, then a part of Germany, where he spent the next eight years working first for de Dietrich, then for Emil Mathis, and finally for Deutz of Cologne.

So far as we can tell, the prototype 3-litre car did not go into production, and we do not know what happened to it. The demand was for larger, more powerful cars capable of hauling heavy coachwork and several passengers. A few months after arriving at Niederbronn Ettore evidently produced the 5.3-litre chassis described in the press in April 1903. This seems to be, and probably was, a development of the first prototype in much of its detail, Ettore now showing for the first time a conservative streak in his design philosophy – if a scheme or layout works well, retain it, or scale it to new requirements. This philosophy stood him in good stead for years, alternated with lateral excursions into the unknown.

Construction of new cars could in those days be completed at a speed that today seems impossible, and we know that Ettore drove a 20-hp de Dietrich car in the Frankfurt race in September 1902. It is therefore probable

that this was his first production for the Baron under the June contract, and the press reference to the event is probably the first time Bugatti's name appears formally on a car as the 'de Dietrich Bugatti'.

In 1903 Ettore produced a car intended for the Paris-Madrid race of that year, but his entry was refused on the grounds that the car was unsafe, the driver being at the rear, over the wheels, and the whole car 'too low'! The race itself was a disaster, and was officially stopped at Bordeaux after numerous fatal accidents.

Yet another version of the normal 30-hp chassis appeared in 1904, and was offered for sale in Britain as a 'Burlington', although there is no evidence of any being sold. However, at about this time de Dietrich decided to give up automobile manufacture and released Ettore. The de Dietrich agent in Strasbourg was Emil Mathis, who had become friendly with Ettore, and it was natural enough for the two of them to enter into partnership to produce Bugatti-Mathis cars, to be sold under the name 'Hermes'. Ettore moved to Strasbourg in 1904 and set up a drawing office, the cars being built in the nearby village of Graffenstaden.

*Typical of the period, a de Dietrich Bugatti in touring form with Ettore at the wheel, accompanied by his friend Emil Mathis, with whom he subsequently went into partnership.*

The Hermes car was produced in several variants, the overall conception of a four-cylinder engine with chain rear drive being as before. A novelty, however, was the camshaft in the bottom of the engine, operating the valves by pull-rods as opposed to push-rods. As before, the cylinders were cast in pairs.

The Mathis-Bugatti agreement lasted from 1904 to 1906, although the two seem to have remained friendly for some time, entering competitions and trials together. Car manufacture was no doubt risky and perhaps unprofitable, at least on the scale achieved by Mathis. There was a recession in the market, and the industry as a whole was depressed.

Ettore now set up as a consulting designer and succeeded in obtaining a contract to design vehicles for the old-established Deutz Gas Engine Company in Cologne. This required him to move with his team of draughtsmen to Cologne, but he retained the right to work on his own designs.

At Deutz he produced two chassis, a large 10-litre chain drive version, and in 1909 a more elegant 3.2-litre car, with for the first time a normal bevel-drive rear axle. Both engines had overhead camshafts and were exceptionally well thought out, especially that for the smaller 1909 car.

There had always been an interest in racing circles in the smaller sort of car, and special 'voiturette' races had been organised, but these had evidently not been of much interest to Ettore. In 1908, however, something happened to change this. At the 1908 Coupe des Voiturettes at Dieppe there appeared three pretty 1.2-litre (62 × 100mm) four-cylinder Isotta-Fraschini cars, delightful machines compared with many of the strange voiturettes typical of the period. The layout and execution of these cars was sufficiently close to a later Bugatti design for it often to be suggested that they were in fact designed by him, but it is certain that this was not so, their designer being a certain Cattaneo, who denied the story when questioned about it before his death. There was, however, an industrial connection between the de Dietrich and Isotta-Fraschini companies, the latter being based in Milan, and a much more tenable argument is that Ettore had some opportunity of seeing the cars.

Ettore, who would never admit to copying, always argued for observation. 'Powers of observation are

*A works picture of the chassis of the Bugatti-designed Mathis car of 1905, sold under the name 'Hermes', in the Graffenstaden factory. It has four cylinders cast in pairs and chain drive.*

indispensible in order to produce anything,' he wrote. 'It is by observation that one can penetrate into the nature of things . . . faster progress would be made in all fields if conceit did not cause us to forget or disdain work done by others before us.'

An entirely logical conclusion is that Ettore saw the Issota-Fraschini chassis, was struck by it, and realised the commercial possibilities of a production car on the same lines. He then went home to his drawing office in Cologne and got busy on his own version, his first 'Pur Sang' car, and the car that was later to establish him as a car manufacturer of exceptional merit.

In broad specification, indeed, the cars were identical: four cylinders (62 × 100mm) in a single-piece cast-iron block, bevel-gear-driven overhead valves, cast aluminium crankcase, separate four-speed gearbox, normal rear axle, and the same wheelbase and track. But the detail is entirely different. Ettore's prototype car, probably correctly known as the Type 10 Bugatti, was built in his cellar in Cologne in 1908–9, while he was designing the second 3.2-litre Deutz model. Indeed, similarities of conception if not of scale can be seen in these two cars. At the end of 1909 Ettore 'took the plunge' with the help of a banker friend and opened his own works in a disused dye factory at Molsheim, a pleasant small town at the north end of the 'Route du Vin' in Alsace, near Strasbourg. In 1910 five cars were produced and sold, and the firm of Ettore Bugatti–Automobiles exhibited at the 1910 Paris Salon. The car was an instant success and 75 were made in 1911.

The engine of the production model was enlarged slightly to 65 × 100mm (1327cc) and versions with a longer wheelbase were soon produced to take four-passenger coachwork. The model (the Type 13) evolved with time and remained in production until 1925, interrupted by war, with developments taking place in various components. The engine had a one-piece block with integral cylinder head, initially with two valves per cylinder, later four, the valves being operated via a bevel-gear-driven overhead camshaft through banana-shaped tappets sliding in arcuate holes in blocks in the 'cam box'. The crank had three bearings, first in bronze, then white metal, and eventually some were ball races; big-end bearings were lubricated first by splash and later by jets.

The clutch was a toggle-operated multi-disc design invented for Deutz and used up to about 1935. The

*Above: Ettore surveys his first 'Pur Sang' car, the Type 10 prototype, built in his cellar in Cologne in 1908. Below: the engine of the Type 10 showing the bevel-driven overhead camshaft and the valves operated by banana-shaped tappets.*

gearbox was separate, in a wide casting bridging the chassis frame, with four speeds and what is known as a 'high-speed layshaft'. This means that the normal constant-mesh gears are at the rear of the box, with the layshaft rotating above engine speed; the advantage of this is that the rotational mass to be accelerated or decelerated when changing gear is greatly reduced compared with a normal gearbox, resulting in those pre-synchromesh days in a very easy, noise-free gearchange. Whether this was the result of Bugatti's observation or a piece of lateral thinking is not known, but the layout has since been reinvented.

The rear axle was of simple bevel type, three-quarters floating and conceptually identical to all Bugatti rear axles used up to 1940. Brakes, typically for the period, worked shoes on the rear wheels, with a foot-operated transmission brake behind the gearbox. Steering was by screw and nut, with a robust and straightforward linkage. The frame was well braced (by contemporary standards) and springs were semi-elliptic all round and relatively long and flexible. In 1913 Bugatti introduced his famous reversed quarter-elliptic springs at the rear, and continued to use this system up to 1940.

On the road the car was a delight and set new standards of handling. A British journalist who tested it in 1910 extolled its virtues: 'It was wonderfully quick in acceleration, absolutely silent on low gears, while the changes were made without a click being heard . . . it is as fast as any of the larger mounts, and in traffic it is quicker because of its handiness. Its upkeep is a mere trifle . . .' Bugatti translated this in his first published catalogue at the end of 1910 as a *'plaisantrie'*. The car was indeed an early Mini-Cooper!

Ettore continued to race cars himself, and to enter for hill climbs, but he used large 5-litre cars, the first of which seems to have been a Deutz used in the Prince Henri Trials in 1909 and then re-engined and modified at Molsheim, with a new cylinder head using two inlet valves and one exhaust valve per cylinder, a construction Ettore was to use up to 1930. A small number of the large cars was made and two or three were sold.

The small car was raced in the small-car class in the 1911 French Grand Prix, and the larger one was entered unsuccessfully at Indianapolis in 1914. Many successes were obtained in sprints and hill climbs by both models, the publicity value of competitive appearances being well recognised by the 'Patron', and fully recorded each year in his catalogues.

War interrupted production of the eight-valve car in August 1914, about 350 in all having been produced pre-war. Examples had been exported widely in Europe, even to Moscow, and to the USA, and they were well received everywhere. When production resumed after the war, so did racing, the first success being at Le Mans in 1920 in the Voiturette race (the car now having the 16-valve cylinder block), and a sensational success was achieved at Brescia in 1921, with the capture of the first four places and record speeds.

We know that Ettore, once established as a manufacturer of successful light cars, still had his eye on larger models to widen his market. He had produced eight and 16-cylinder

*In the 1922 French Grand Prix at Strasbourg, Ettore's long-tailed, cowled 8-cylinder cars were no stranger-looking than the Ballots, one of which is shown on the left of this picture.*

aero-engines during the war and turned to this 'straight eight' layout for a larger car in 1920, exhibiting an unfinished 3-litre car at the Paris and London shows.

It was too soon for him to have the resources to develop and produce such a vehicle, and a more modest programme saw the production of a 2-litre eight-cylinder engine to be fitted to the four-cylinder touring car chassis (now known as the Brescia after its racing success). The new car – the Type 30 – appeared at the 1922 shows, and went into production in 1923.

Three racing versions of the eight-cylinder car appeared at the 1922 French Grand Prix, run nearby at Strasbourg. They performed creditably against opposition from Italy, Britain and elsewhere in France. Less successful was a foray in 1923 to Indianapolis, the chassis now fitted with single-seat bodies. Only one car out of five finished, the others having relatively serious mechanical problems illustrating some inherent weaknesses of Ettore's mechanical design.

For the 1923 French Grand Prix at Tours, Bugatti produced a remarkable 'tank' car, of a supposedly aerodynamic, all-enveloping design, more likely as a result of some free-thinking than from observation. This used his relatively successful eight-cylinder 2-litre engine (with earlier bearing weaknesses now overcome by the use of ball and roller bearings) in a box-like body with a very short (2-metre) wheelbase and a quasi-aerofoil side elevation. This was ranged alongside an even more strange-looking car from the aeroplane designer Voisin, and a number of relatively conventional and good-looking cars from Sunbeam, Delage and Rolland-Pilain. The press reception of the strange 'beetles' from Bugatti and Voisin was not good: 'nightmarish monsters' was a typical comment, and this was not alleviated by the leading Bugatti arriving third, behind two Sunbeams, 25 minutes after Segrave in the winning car.

Ettore must have gone home from Tours disappointed at the poor showing of his car, still smarting from the

disasters at Indianapolis, and certainly stimulated, whether consciously or subconsciously, by the Fiats, Sunbeams and even the Rolland-Pilains from the Grand Prix. The lack of press eulogy would not have helped his ego.

Something happened that winter to change his whole approach to racing-car design; we do not know what for sure, except that it was to have a profound significance for the future course of his work and his productions. Up to that moment his chassis design had been excellent, elegantly conventional in the main, and his personal interest in new design had been in the engine. He had proven and excellent clutches, gearboxes and rear axles, all of which had virtually been designed in 1908 or 1910. He knew he had an eight-cylinder engine that was reasonably powerful and which, if he could solve its bearing problems, should also be reliable.

What he lacked, or had not bothered to achieve, was a decent-looking vehicle. The successful four-cylinder Brescia model, winning races and hill climbs all over the world, was an ugly duckling of a car, not even particularly well finished. The eight-cylinder engine was handsome enough, with its narrow rectangular lines which appealed to the artist's eye; but the eight-cylinder chassis in racing trim could not compare with the competition.

It seems to this writer that the most likely cause of his change of thinking came from the 1923 Fiat racing car, the 805, which appeared first at Tours (unsuccessfully), and a few weeks later won at Monza for the Italian (and that year's European) Grand Prix. Fiat had already beaten

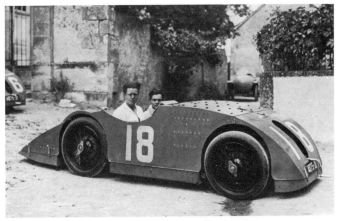

*The strange 'tank' car which Ettore produced for the 1923 Grand Prix at Tours foreshadowed later aerodynamic designs but was unsuccessful. Prince de Cystria is at the wheel.*

*Left: the 8-valve Type 13 Bugatti was the direct development of the Type 10 prototype, being produced (with changes) from 1910 to 1925, and having a 16-valve head from 1920. It set new standards of handling and established Ettore as a manufacturer of light cars.*

*Below: the Type 35B Bugatti racing car of 1926 followed the lines of Ettore's eight-cylinder masterpiece, the Type 35 of 1924, very closely, but had a supercharged engine, increased in size to 2.3 litres. A modified twin-overhead-camshaft cylinder construction was introduced in 1931 for the Type 51. These cars were among the most successful in motor racing history.*

*Right: the Type 59 Bugatti of 1933, with its 3.3-litre supercharged engine based on the Type 57 touring car, was the ultimate expression of the theme set by Ettore, but its conception owed a great deal to the skill of his son Jean. It is seen here alongside its Type 35 predecessor.*

*Below: the Type 57 'Atalante' fixed-head, two-seater coupé designed by Jean Bugatti was one of half a dozen models produced by him for this chassis in the mid 1930s.*

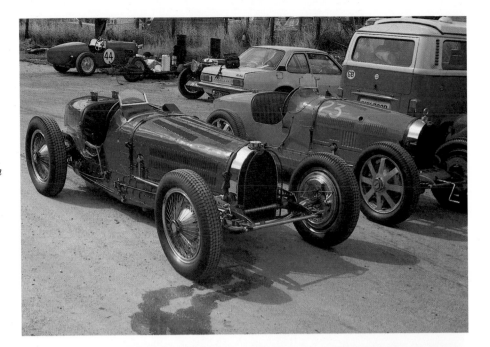

Ettore in 1922 at Monza, and he knew it was not sensible to enter the unhappy tank cars there in 1923. What his Italian *confrères* from Turin could do, could not he? He did not agree with their use of a supercharger on the engine, but he could acknowledge the aesthetic appeal of their handsome 805, and much of its detail. He could appreciate their mechanical front brakes, but could think of a simpler way of doing it, to replace his relatively unreliable hydraulic ones. He liked the way the Fiat body and chassis frame swept in at the rear to give a good shape to the tail. And in particular his eye noted the elegant front axle, hollow and with holes in it through which the springs passed. If it were split in the middle to allow it to be hollowed out, could he not think of a way to have an axle that was hollow in the middle and closed at both ends?

There seems little doubt that in the winter of 1923–4 Ettore did some hard thinking, even unconsciously turning over a new leaf. All the cars he produced from then on were aesthetically delightful, all were eye-catching, and the designer's attempts at treating the external appearance as well as the mechanical detail of each one were apparent.

In April 1924 he wrote to his friend and faithful customer Junek in Prague, sending him the sketch of what the 1924 car was to look like. 'Springs and so on are completely within the body works,' he wrote. 'The under part of the car is completely straight, only the cooling ribs project through. The front axle is a mechanical masterpiece. It is a hollow axle of quite new construction.' Later he explained that he had abandoned the thick aerofoil body used on the tank cars 'in spite of its technical advantages, simply with the object of obtaining a more elegant shape, to facilitate sales'.

The 1924 car, the Type 35 Bugatti, was the result, perhaps the best-looking of all racing cars, and a technical and aesthetic *tour de force*. This is not the place to describe the car in detail, except to draw attention to particular elements or features.

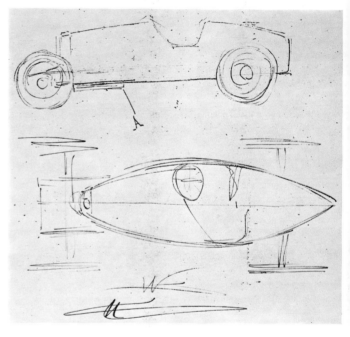

*Above: the sketch of the 1924 car, the Type 35, which Ettore sent his friend Junek. Left: the handsome 2-litre Fiat 805 of 1923 was the car that inspired Ettore's masterpiece.*

The overall lines are very fine, the balance of position of wheels, radiator, cockpit and tail are near if not absolute perfection. If one contemplates the bodywork, bonnet, scuttle, tail, undertray and fairings it is difficult to suggest the slightest improvement. The affinity between the draughtsman's pencil and the panel-beater's hammer in defining and flowing one shape into another is immediately apparent.

The engineering detail too is excellent, subject to some criticisms to be advanced later. The front axle combines lightness and strength in bending and torsion in its tubular construction, the ends being forged solid to form the kingpin eyes after boring through. The passing of the springs through the axle eliminates an unhappy offset and lowers the chassis height. The axle's polished smoothness contrasts with the earlier die-forged H-section used by Ettore.

The cable-operated brakes are extremely effective, geometrically correct, and have the subtle feature at the front that, by being disposed above the axle centre line, axle twist on braking provides the front brakes with positive feedback or servo action (very effective with 1924 brakes, but rather too effective with the enlarged brakes used by 1934).

The eight-spoked cast and weight-saving aluminium wheels, with integral well cooled brake drums, were a much noted feature of the car, and in practice a source of speculation when continuous tyre trouble (not in fact related to the wheel construction) caused the cars' failure in the Lyons Grand Prix, where they first appeared. A

*Top: Ettore is the centre of attraction at the Lyons Grand Prix of 1924 with his new beauty, though tyre trouble in the race prevented the new cars' success.*

*Right: during the race, Garnier leads another Bugatti at the Esses.*

Bugatti innovation in 1924, cast wheels are now commonplace. A detail feature of the early wheels, which used the so-called straight-sided or beaded edge tyres, was a restraining band that clamped between the tyre beads inside the wheel – another Bugatti novelty reinvented since.

The 2-litre engine was as before, except that it now had a full ball and roller bearing crankshaft – a remarkable production built up from many pieces and capable of being dismantled and reassembled while remaining in balance and truth. If Ettore could not understand how to design proper plain oil-lubricated bearings, he could at least get round the problem by using rollers.

The magneto was mounted on the dash, protected from the weather and engine heat. The dash carried only essential instruments, but a clock was included for the benefit of drivers in a five-hour Grand Prix. The steering wheel was wood-rimmed in walnut, and as pleasing to hold as to look at. The steering of the car was superb, with the front wheels clearly visible from the driving seat so that one could drive on the proverbial sixpence. Before the days of 'over' or 'understeering', drift angles and side-slip, the car could be placed and cornered to perfection.

Although tyre troubles at the 1924 French Grand Prix prevented success, a month later the car did well in Spain, and from 1925 until about 1930 it swept most if not all before it, establishing itself as the most successful of all early racing cars, only recently yielding pride of place to Ferrari and Lotus. Year by year the model developed, with a supercharger being added in 1926, the engine enlarged to

2.3 litres (the Type 35B), and a modified twin-overhead-camshaft cylinder construction in 1931 (the model then being designated Type 51). Visually the car remained the same, except that the radiator and tyre section became larger, and only the knowledgeable can distinguish a 1924 model from a 1931.

Inevitably, simplified, lower-cost versions were produced, some with the eight-cylinder racing engine, some with a new four-cylinder engine (Type 37). A total of 16 cars was delivered in 1924, about 90 in 1925 and no less than 250 of all versions in 1926, with a peak monthly output of 32 cars in June 1926. Total production of the full-race version was no less than 350, together with about 300 of the sport versions – a remarkable output.

Customers were delighted with their cars and did not fail to write to Ettore to say so.

Mr Bertrand from Barcelona wrote in December 1924: 'It is a veritable jewel . . . my trip was triumphal, at Barcelona wild success . . .'

Member of Parliament Sir Robert Bird of Solihull (who took delivery of the Olympia Show car) wrote at Christmas 1924: 'what satisfaction I have from my "little blue phenomenon" . . . this thoroughbred of thorough-breds . . .'

Lady Cholmondley wrote from London in March 1925: '. . . it is a joy to drive, and I am astonished with the results from the point of view of speed, and acceleration, all achieved with complete safety . . .'

Mr Aisman-Ferry wrote in April 1925: 'I am really enchanted with the car which is the mechanical perfection of the century.'

Even a competitor to Bugatti, Louis Delage, was generous in his praise: 'Your cars handle so well, and have such acceleration . . .'

If the first sortie of the new Grand Prix car at Lyons had not been successful, it soon fulfilled its promise, and in 1926 it won seven major Grands Prix. Admittedly by now

*By 1926 a supercharger had been added to increase the Bugattis' power output, and the radiator was enlarged. Jules Goux at the weigh-in for the San Sebastian race in an eight-cylinder Type 39A.*

Ettore had had to eat his earlier words and add the supercharger that the engine needed to keep ahead of the competition from Alfa Romeo and Delage. He had to enlist the help of a specialist designer to deal with the internal details of the Roots blower he adopted, his powers of observation now failing him.

By 1930 his engine needed more drastic redesign to increase power and make full use of the alcohol-based fuels that were now commonly used for racing. It was Ettore's son Jean who persuaded him to copy an American Miller cylinder head construction, which provided another 25 or 30 horsepower. Finally, the ultimate Bugatti Grand Prix car was the 3.3-litre Type 59 of 1933, but this is perhaps more to the credit of Ettore's son Jean than to the father, and will be referred to later.

There seems little doubt that Ettore's personality developed as a result of his early success, at the age of 20, in designing a successful motor car without recourse to theoretical training and study. He would have been less than human if his ego had not been inflated by these events, by widespread public acclaim, and subsequently by being provided with the opportunity to design car after car.

It is therefore to be expected that he should cover up his lack of technical expertise by a reserve, by being dogmatic or at least authoritarian, and by the use of his declared powers of observation, rather than by the sort of technical debate other designers and engineers find stimulating and productive. A degree of conservatism in his thinking would hide a reluctance to enter fields he could not understand. We know, for example, that he resisted the use of front wheel brakes for some time, subsequently coming out with a brilliantly simple solution that may well have originated with one of his draughtsmen. Many other faults in his designs had to await the day when the son could try his hand, and the father could take a pride in Jean's frequently successful achievements.

His personality and his business or marketing methods created a mystique that he exploited to the full, either consciously or unconsciously. While the tradition of the *Patron* in France and Germany is stronger than in Britain or the USA, it is remarkable that at no time at Molsheim was any other personality (apart from his son) allowed to develop. Ettore had many able and competent collaborators, all of whom were anonymous, except

Costantini, the Italian count who looked after racing, and Pracht the accountant. And it is said that only Costantini was ever on the familiar second-person terms so usual in French with Ettore.

He had many acquaintances – the number of those who knew him grows annually! – but evidently few personal friends outside his family. We have warm personal correspondence from his early admirer Dr Espanet, a French Air Force pilot who met him first at the 1910 Automobile Salon and later went to test his engines in the air with Duesenberg in the USA in 1918; but even Espanet moved to the employee category when he ran the Paris Service Depot in 1939 and then after the war. Jules Goux, the famous racing driver, who drove for Bugatti in the mid-1920s and then joined the staff at Molsheim, was still the employee to Mr Bugatti.

His family life with his children, and a wife who remained in the background, was happy. He loved his horses, and would as soon show you his stables as his racing cars, although the latter were not neglected for the potential customer. There are many stories of generosity, and special prices for drivers whom he liked; Mr Farr of Edinburgh has recounted how as a young engineering student, writing for a crankshaft replacement for an old Brescia model and mentioning his lack of finance, he received a new one with compliments, a note attached '*moi aussi étais apprenti*' – 'I also was an apprentice'.

His personality as we have said had been influenced by his early success; shyness must have developed from his lack of technical training, turning into an aloofness which avoided questioning.

Who but Bugatti could write to a customer, as he did in 1924 to Sir Robert Bird: 'I am absolutely astonished to learn that you have decided to fit lamps to your car . . . I learn also that you propose to change the carburetters . . . I am opposed to any modifications . . .'

Treatment such as this seems to have enhanced his relationship with his many well-to-do customers; it certainly encouraged stories, probably untrue, of particular incidents – his answer to someone who complained about his car's brakes ('I design my cars to go, not to stop'), or that it was difficult to start in winter ('Get a heated garage').

Ettore clearly had little interest in finance, yet seems to have survived surprisingly well, aided no doubt by the

*The magnificent hand-finished engine of the monster 12-litre Royale – the car of Kings which no King ever had. Only six of these huge cars were ever made, and only three of these were sold.*

faithful Pracht. He spent large sums on racing, and also indeed on abortive racing models such as the experimental 16-cylinder car and a pair of four-wheel-drive cars. The high selling price of the racing models, which were actually little more expensive to build than the touring versions, helped. The substantial expenditure by racing drivers on overhaul work at the factory, and the high cost of spares – willingly bought because they were genuine – undoubtedly also contributed.

What seem absurd in retrospect are some of the design fantasies he indulged in, or perhaps could not prevent his fertile brain from producing: an eight-engined boat to cross the Atlantic in 50 hours in 1927; aero engines in 1923, to say nothing of a complete fighter aeroplane in 1939 (but this had some assistance from the French Government). The worst fantasy of all became a reality – the design and production of the enormous 12-litre 'Royale' cars, of which only six were ever made, and only three sold. But another idea became a great success – the design of high-speed railcars for the French railways, which made use of the excellent large engine he had produced for the ill-fated Royale.

No review of Ettore's work would be complete without some comments on his successful car designs from an engineering point of view. The cars in fact succeeded in spite of certain technical faults, which may perhaps be illustrated by discussing two areas.

First, Bugatti's classic cylinder construction with three vertical valves per cylinder. The cylinder and head are the real heart of any internal combustion engine. It is here that an explosive gas is compressed and burnt to produce power. The more readily the gas can be introduced and evacuated, and the more even the heat distribution, the better the engine will perform. Ettore could be forgiven for any design he adopted at the beginning of the century, as knowledge was limited and he had little to 'observe'; but this could not apply after 1918.

Ettore believed in the importance of exhausting the products of combustion rapidly: his exhaust valves were large and his exhaust pipework was excellent. But he was not so seized with the importance of filling the cylinders with fresh charge from the carburetter, although he did understand the need to heat the incoming charge when using the heavy, non-volatile fuel of the day.

Jean Bugatti with one of the most beautiful cars ever made – the roadster Royale which he designed for Mr Esders in 1932. The owner did not drive at night and so needed no headlamps. Rembrandt's elephant mascot is just visible on the radiator.

Another Bugatti fantasy was the eight-engined ship designed by Ettore for the transatlantic route. It was never built.

In the 1930s the Molsheim factory was much occupied, as was Ettore himself, with the production of excellent high-speed railcars for the French railways, using the engines from the ill-fated Royale car.

The four-valve cylinder construction he introduced in the Brescia model had the advantage of relatively good breathing, as there was adequate space round the valves to allow the gas to enter or escape when they were opened. Simple calculation will show that, to provide the same area through an open valve as is provided in the throat passage, a valve requires a lift of about one quarter of the valve throat diameter, and a clearance all round the valve comparable to the lift (or say at least two thirds of it) if the flow of gas is not to be obstructed by the cylinder head or wall. If the Brescia was not bad in this respect, most other Bugatti designs were deficient – especially the later (but successful) single camshaft engines.

During the 1914–18 war, Bugatti had occupied himself by designing aero-engines, the 16-cylinder version being taken up by the American Government and produced by the Duesenberg Company, though the war came to an end before the engine went into service. The US Government engaged Col C King to 'redesign the engine for production', much to Ettore's irritation. But the changes made by King were all good ones and designed to eliminate the inherent weaknesses of Bugatti's layout, based on the three-valve scheme used in the 1912 5-litre car.

To put this aero-engine into perspective it is necessary to look at its competitors. The Hispano-Suiza engine designed by Marc Birkigt was the outstandingly effective and successful engine used by the Allies. This had a cylinder liner in steel, with a blind end, bored for the ports for inlet and exhaust valves with either two or four valves per cylinder. This liner was screwed into an aluminium casting with its own water jacket, the ports in the liner registering with the valve seat holes in the dry liner. Water leaks were few, but it was reported that valve grinding was frequently needed, no doubt due to poor heat transfer between the valve seats and the aluminium 'head'. The overhead camshaft operated directly on the ends of the valves and the valve guides were screwed in, in best Bugatti practice! On the other hand there was ample space around the valves to allow free entry to the mixture.

Birkigt and Bugatti might both have had a look at the contemporary German Mercedes aero-engine, which was similar in conception to the sensational 1914 racing-car engine that had won the French Grand Prix, although it is probably more correct to say that the racing car was based on the aero-engine. This was an excellent design with inclined valves, well guided valves operated through rockers from a single overhead camshaft, and with adequate gas passages. The welded or brazed sheet-metal water jacketing was perhaps not to Ettore's liking, being expensive and complicated when used with a cast cylinder.

To be fair to Ettore, even if he had had a chance to study the Mercedes engine, he might not have appreciated its virtues as its specific output was not all that high. The 1912 Peugeot Grand Prix engine had produced 17 horsepower per litre, and the 1914 Mercedes winner just 25. The slower aero-engine however only managed 12 hp/litre, whereas Hispano and Rolls-Royce were soon up to 20 hp/litre, and Ettore set out to get a little more than this from his 16-cylinder aero-engine. At the end of the war the Napier Lion engine pointed the way ahead with an excellent 37 hp/litre, which the racing-car designers only exceeded in 1922.

Col King did not like some of the detail design of Bugatti's engine, for example the lack of water cooling around the valve seats, and he altered the cylinder casting to improve matters. Nor did he like the aluminium closing plate on top of the block, a feature Ettore introduced on the aero-engine and retained in his car engines up to 1932. Threaded valve guides, as used by Hispano and Bugatti, were rightly not considered good practice, and Col King used plain pressed-in ones. But he could do little to improve the breathing of the engine, with its vertical valves, pitched closely together.

Some correspondence between King and Bugatti, which still exists, shows how strongly Ettore objected to the changes to his design, but his counter-arguments were largely emotional and he did not – or perhaps could not – produce engineering reasons for leaving the design in its original form.

The second aspect of Bugatti's engineering relates to lubrication. The reader may forgive the reminder that there are two basic types of lubrication, called boundary layer and hydrodynamic, respectively. The first relies on a feed of oil being introduced by some means, including the action of gravity or capillary action, between two moving surfaces to separate them. Fairly thick oil is an advantage in this case and castor oil is the supreme lubricant for such duty if it is warm enough. Modern lubrication, however, uses the dynamic self-pumping action of oil supplied under pressure at the right place in a journal bearing to keep the

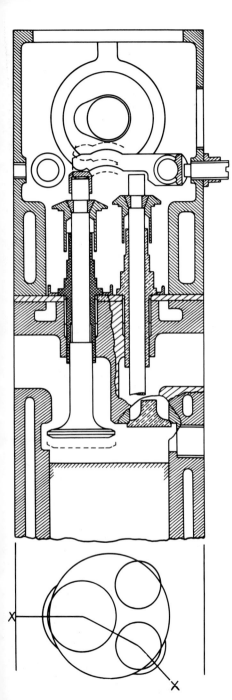

Cylinder head construction compared. Left: Bugatti's three-valve layout, based on his 1912 design, had relatively poor breathing. Centre: the Hispano-Suiza was the most successful aero-engine design used by the Allies in the First World War. Right: the advanced inclined-valve layout used in the sensational German Mercedes racing car of 1914.

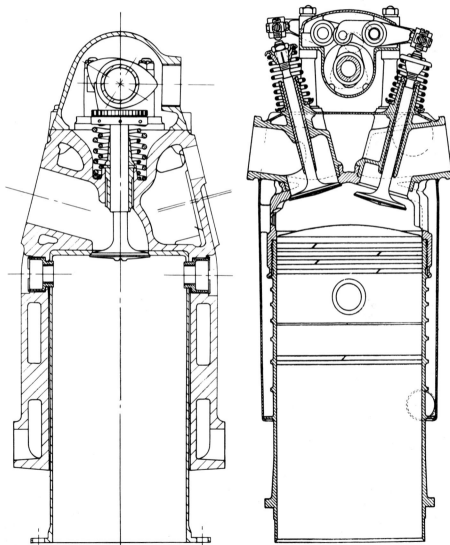

two parts separated and spinning freely; thin oil in large volume is needed and this conducts away the heat of friction. A hydrodynamic bearing will carry a much greater load at a higher speed than the earlier drip-fed or squirt-lubricated type.

Ettore himself used simple lubrication systems on all his designs until forced to change by events about 1929 (and one wonders whether he was not pushed to change by his son). At high speed, under sustained track conditions, bearings overheated and failed. Only conversion to roller bearings could overcome this weakness.

It would not be practicable to 'observe' how to redesign a lubrication system; it would have to be studied from a theoretical base, which Ettore did not have. When a bearing failed on a Bugatti engine, it could be blamed on bad maintenance, dirty oil, or a piece of rag in one of the many small jets in the lubrication system!

But if some of Ettore's engineering is poor, much of his design is superb. Design in this context means not only aesthetic appearance and overall shape and form, but detailed mechanical and structural solutions, right down to a nut and bolt. We can choose many examples, starting with the simplest.

*Nuts and bolts.* After 1923 Ettore started to use his own design of nut and bolt, incidentally using odd metric diameters (5, 7, 9, 11mm) rather than the normal 6, 8, 10, 12mm. The bolt has a square head, to encourage one to hold rather than turn it, and the nut has an integral washer. These nuts were expensive, as the hexagon had to be milled, rather than being made from hexagonal bar, but the integral washer meant that the nut was less likely to come undone under vibration. This feature is now common on special aircraft nuts, but Bugatti was well ahead in 1923.

*Leather.* Ettore was the first to use flexible joints for steering parts and on such couplings as the magneto, the transmission torque arm, or for shock absorbers. Today we use reinforced rubber in place of Ettore's leather.

*Gears.* Ettore seems to have had a first-class understanding of the use of gears and the proper materials for them. His gearbox gears, and the many bevels and skew gears on the engine, are all very well done. The worm and wheel gearing of the later steering gearboxes is impressively effective and robust.

*Magneto drive.* A scroll system to drive a magneto providing a simple advance/retard mechanism was first used on Ettore's wartime aero-engine, and later on the Grand Prix car. It is a delightful three-dimensional device, typical of Ettore's ability to visualise form and making full use of the skilled labour he had available.

*Steering details.* The various steering arms, tapered in section, socketed to hubs with tapered wedge ends, and with one-piece ball ends, are superb details, benefiting from the polishing that is expected on racing-car steering.

*Chassis details.* Items such as the GP starting handle and hand-brake lever are perfectly shaped, with subtle tapers, and are a pleasure to handle and use.

*Materials.* Ettore was generous in his use of nickel chrome steel for many of his parts, and seldom showed any sign of corner-cutting. Chassis fittings such as wing stays and the like provide many examples of fine blacksmith work.

We do not know in detail how far Ettore himself went in preparing layouts of designs that he wanted his drawing office to complete. Right to the end of his life he was sketching on small pads, or sitting at a drawing-board working on 40 × 30inch cartridge paper. Every drawing is initialled and dated, as is every change made later. A designer of his ability, working with a small team of draughtsmen, finds a way of working that uses everyone's talents to the best. There is no doubt that much of the basic layout of his early car designs was produced by Ettore himself, and that he was very well supported by his draughtsmen. Much of the detailed quality of the Type 35 Grand Prix car no doubt came from the work of his colleagues, unfortunately anonymous except for an initial or a name on the drawing – Bertrand, Nuss, Urach, Pichetto . . .

Bugatti engine designs are full of interesting detail, and delight the eye when they are uncovered, like this Type 44. Leather is used for the steering box coupling and the general appearance of the power unit has obviously been carefully considered. Note the spare spark plugs.

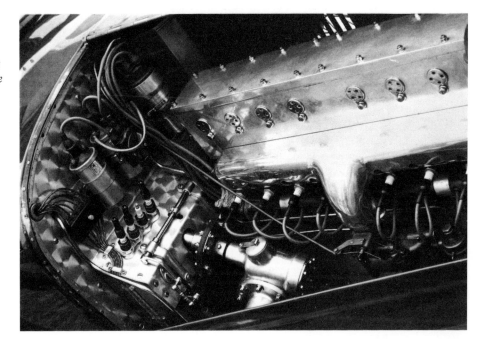

One of Ettore's surviving sketch designs, in this case for cylinder head layout. His practice was to initial and date any worthwhile idea, and any later changes. 'Très bien', he has noted on a detail here.

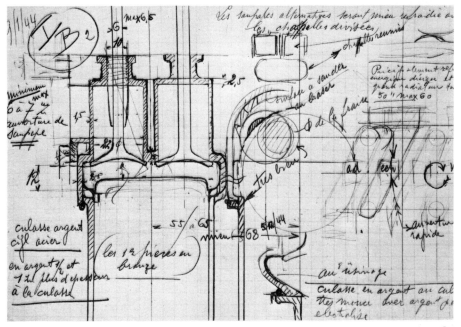

When Jean took over car design in 1930–1, so the habits changed. Jean – imaginative, receptive and creative – was less of a draughtsman, more of an engineer. Ettore turned more and more to his railcars and steam engines, still drawing all the time but less likely to produce the final schemes for the larger and more complex projects he was interested in. And then the war of 1939–45 came, and Ettore had little else to do but scheme away at engines, bicycles, racing cars and machine tools for a post-war programme that did not materialise. His son Jean had left the scene tragically on 11 August 1939.

Perhaps the *Patron* should be allowed his own last word on the importance of drawing and design. 'The drawing-board enables me to see in complete form whatever it is I am about to make, but often I think that one should not put pencil to paper before having visualised what one wants from all angles. Over the years and after much experience of drawing quite novel and complicated things in pocket-books I have come to work by a series of mental images; and the drawing-board enables me to give effect to those images. A technician who cannot put down his ideas on paper is at a great disadvantage. To sum up then – powers of observation and a great facility with the pencil are the two attributes which matter the most.'

BIBLIOGRAPHY

Bradley, W. F. *Ettore Bugatti*. Motor Racing Publications, 1948/1959

Eaglesfield, B. and Hampton, C. W. P. *The Bugatti Book*. London, Motor Racing Publications, 1954

Conway, H. G. *Bugatti – Le Pur Sang des Automobiles*. London, G. T. Foulis, 1963, 1968, 1974

Conway, H. G. *Grand Prix Bugatti*. London, G. T. Foulis, 1968

Dumont, P. *Les 'Pur Sang' de Molsheim*. Paris, 1975

Kestler, P. *Bugatti – L'Evolution d'un Style*. Lausanne, Edita, 1975

Borge, J. and Viasnoff, N. *La Bugatti*. Paris, 1977 (paperback)

Barker, R. *Bugatti*. London, 1971 (paperback)

Bugatti, L'Ebé. *L'Epopée Bugatti*. Paris 1966 (English edition *The Bugatti Story*. London, Souvenir Press, 1967)

Hucke, M. and U. *Bugatti Dokumentation einer Automobile Marke*. Bad Oeyenhausen, 1971, 1976

BIOGRAPHICAL SUMMARY

1881 Born Milan 15 September
1897 Apprenticed Prinetti and Stucchi
1901 Constructed first four-wheeled car and exhibited it in Milan
1902 Married Barbara Bolzoni
     Contracted to de Dietrich and moved to Niederbronn in Alsace-Loraine
1904 Moved to Strasbourg with Mathis
1907 Moved to Cologne to work for Deutz
1908 Designed the Type 10
1910 Opened works at Molsheim
1914 Moved to Milan then Paris
1919 Reopened Molsheim works
1921 Sensational success at Brescia GP
1923 Tank cars at Tours GP
1924 Designed Type 35
1926 Won all major GP races
1931 Type 51
1933 Type 59
1936 Quitted Molsheim following industrial troubles
1946 Married Geneviève Delcuze
1947 Died Paris 21 August

# Jean Bugatti 1909-1939

Hugh Conway

Gianoberto Carlo Rembrandt Ettore Bugatti, whom everyone called Jean, was born during his father's 'Deutz' period at Mülheim-on-Rhine in 1909 and unhappily met his end in a car accident in August 1939, a few days before war was declared in Europe. He was beyond question the most talented of Ettore's four children from his first wife Barbara, demonstrating clearly the artist's eye for line and form and evidently being particularly receptive to technical and engineering experience and opinion. His father became effectively crippled by the 1939 War and its effect on the market for the specialised motor cars he had produced. Had Jean lived he might well have made more sensible and economical attempts to put the Bugatti Company back on its feet at Molsheim

after 1945, although as no other specialist car survived for any length of time after the war it seems unlikely that even he could have succeeded in the prevailing circumstances.

Moving to Milan at the age of six when war came, and then to Paris when his mother joined Ettore there, Jean had a normal schooling in Paris and later in Alsace when the family returned to the factory in 1919. He was 15 when

*Jean's first venture, at the age of about 21, was to lead production of the large 4.9-litre supercharged engine for the Type 50 chassis. A Miller-type cylinder head layout greatly increased the output of the earlier Bugatti engine.*

To many people the most desirable of all Grand Prix cars, the 1931 Type 51 Bugatti, the design of which was probably influenced considerably by Jean. Chiron and Varzi's car is seen here winning the 1931 French Grand Prix at Monthlèry, and lifting a front wheel in the process.

The Type 51 engine was basically that of the original Type 35, with a new cylinder block and camshaft arrangement for better breathing. The sculptural quality of the engine is shown to good effect here.

he joined his happy father in the family caravan which Ettore had set up at Lyons for the Grand Prix in 1924 at which he was making his big effort in the new and much admired Type 35. Jean's formative years were the 'golden years' of the Type 35, during which the Bugatti swept all before it in 1926 and became the Ferrari or Lotus of the late 1920s, winning more races than any other make of car until overtaken recently by these two modern champions. Jean had his father's taste for fine machinery, speed on the road and racing cars, and was soon tearing round the

factory in one car or another until he was old enough to drive whatever car he chose on testing, but not in racing. 'The father refused to allow his son to race. He recognised there only too well the gifts of talent to see them wasted, however compulsive the sporting urge.' (P de Rothschild).

By the end of the 1920s Jean was old enough for his engineering opinions to be listened to. It was perhaps much clearer to him than to the blinkered vision of his older father that the Bugatti racing car in its Type 35 form, with a rectangular, three-valve cylinder head, was not

*Jean in the Type 43 Grand Sport (which he fostered) with his younger brother Roland in the 'Baby' electric replica Bugatti at Molsheim in 1927. Behind are Rembrandt's sculptures.*

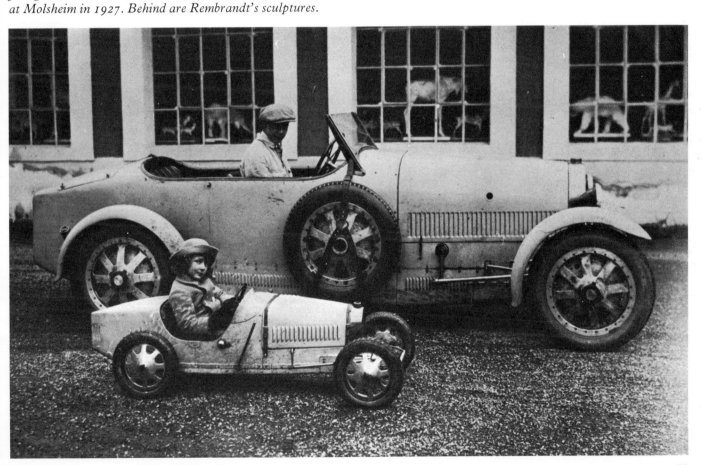

capable of meeting opposition from Italy and elsewhere in the race for power into which all motor racing develops. Although we do not know the inner details of the story, we do know that in 1929 Bugatti arranged an exchange with an American racing driver, Leon Duray, who had come over with a pair of the successful Miller racing cars so popular at Indianapolis to take on the Europeans at Monza and elsewhere. He did not have much success, and at the end of the season found himself in financial difficulties. Under what circumstances we cannot tell (but surely Jean must have had a hand in it), Duray was persuaded to exchange his two Millers for three of the Grand Sport Type 43 Bugattis which the factory had in stock, unsold – it was not a good time for selling the fastest and one of the most expensive sports cars in the world. Duray returned to the USA and sold the cars, no doubt at a good price – they are still in existence and much treasured.

The Bugatti drawing office set about drawing out the

heart of the Miller engine, the cylinder block and valve/camshaft arrangement. Jean knew well enough that this was far superior to the existing Bugatti layout from the point of view of power. Had his father been a little more receptive he might have realised years before that the layout of the Miller engine owed much in turn to earlier successful French Peugeot, Ballot and Delage designs.

The first version of the new engine layout that evolved through copying the Miller design was a 4.9-litre engine made by altering the cylinder head arrangement of the existing luxury car known as the Type 46, the new car being designated Type 50. It was supercharged, expensive, clad in impressive coachwork from the best of French coachbuilders, and was much photographed with mannequins with flowing dresses and large hats at *concours d'élégance*. Distinguished, and of necessity wealthy, Frenchmen bought it, and found it comfortable but dangerously powerful and fast; indeed, the London

*A superb example of the 'razor-edge' or Fiacre-style body on a 5.3-litre Type 46 chassis. Both Ettore and Jean favoured this elegant style.*

representative of the Bugatti factory was reluctant to import it because he thought it unsafe.

Jean was about 21 at this time. Before he was 22 he was allowed to apply the new (Miller!) layout to the ageing Type 35 Grand Prix car; no doubt his father could remember what he himself had achieved by that age. The new racing car was known as the Type 51, following Bugatti's numbering sequence, and was probably the best of all Bugatti racing cars. Only the expert can recognise the subtle external differences between the Type 35 and its final form and the later Type 51, as only detailed modifications were needed to the chassis, axles and gearbox, and none at all to the overall shape and appearance of the car. The new conversion cylinder block and head with its two overhead camshafts produced 25 or more extra horsepower, which gave the car the necessary new lease of life that the chassis as a whole deserved.

The car had a very good start by winning the Monaco Grand Prix in 1931 and continued with great success for several years until the German government-sponsored Auto-Union and Mercedes racers took over towards the end of the decade. Jean was allowed later to compete against these larger cars with some success, as we will see.

Although Jean at the age of 21 was allowed to influence Molsheim engine design and later to take over responsibility for production models from about 1935 to 1939 as well as the racing programme, it is as a coachwork designer that his talent is most clearly evidenced.

The production of specialised one-off or small series car bodies is today a thing of the past, kept alive by enthusiast craftsmen with well-to-do customers for replica vintage car bodies, able to pay for thousands of hours of skilled joinery, sheet-metal work and upholstery. In 1930 it was a thriving industry of well known names that are perhaps forgotten by today's generation: Weymann, Van den Plas, Saoutchick, Figoni-Falaschi, Park Ward, James Young,

*Jean originated the streamlined 'Profilée' bodies produced in two versions on the 4.9 litre chassis, one as here with a sweeping tail, the other truncated.*

Mulliner, Gangloff. . . . Construction was not difficult, merely laborious. Chassis makers would deliver a chassis to the coachbuilder in running order, with a bulkhead and fully instrumented dashboard already in place. Longitudinal wood members in ash were laid on the chassis frame and frames were built up and across, with the joints mortised and plated with steel (with flexibility in the case of Weymann, since his bodies were to be fabric covered). Each body frame was made to fit a particular chassis. The coachbuilder was allowed to drill holes in the chassis frame to attach his body, but was encouraged to put these in the vertical webs of frame members if possible, which it often was not. Blacksmiths would attend to hand-forge iron – not steel – wing stays and running-board brackets, often with elegant results if the stays were to show. Then the body frame would be removed from the chassis for the attention of sheet-metal workers who, working generally in steel, but often in soft aluminium

sheet, would cover the body frame and doors. Tooling was minimal, and certainly there were no dies such as are used in the construction of a modern pressed-steel car body.

Most people watching a good sheet-metal worker in a body shop, or today more likely in an aircraft factory, will marvel at the way the skilled craftsman will flow the metal with roll, hammer, dolly and former into the most intricate three-dimensional shapes. These men are artists, with the artist's eye for shape and form. The metal flows into even, smooth shapes, and from the simplest sketch of what is wanted the skilled worker can produce the most aesthetically satisfying results.

It seems clear that Ettore Bugatti himself had little interest in bodywork, at least until 1924 when, as we have recounted, he changed direction and produced (or saw produced?) the lovely Type 35. Jean was 15 at the time and it seems unlikely that he had any direct influence on the change, although we cannot be sure; a word from a son of

*The truncated variant of the 'Profilée' body style can be compared with that on the previous page.*

*Right: Jean in his own Bugatti roadster with Totosche, the Sicilian donkey given to his father Ettore by Count Florio after winning the Targa Florio race for the third time.*

*Below: another roadster, the American-style Type 40A. The two-tone paintwork on the panel-beaten body mouldings is clearly visible.*

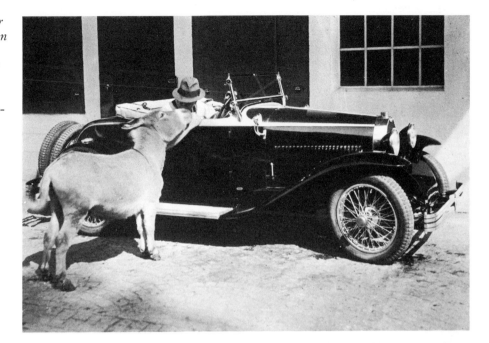

15 can influence a headstrong father where an outsider would fail.

In any event, the Bugatti works opened a body shop to make coachwork other than that for Grand Prix cars some time around 1927 or 1928. The first efforts seem to have been concentrated on the Grand Sport version of the racing car, the Type 43, which used the supercharged racing engine in a longer wheelbase chassis and was put on the market in 1927 as the world's fastest and first 100mph sports car – which indeed it was. This was illustrated by

the factory, with some justice, as a three-and-a-half-seater, meaning that the rear seats were really only suitable for two small young ladies – what today we call with more tact a 'two plus two'. The lines of this car seem even today to be more or less perfect, certainly in side elevation, and the similarity to the Grand Prix car is clear.

If Jean had no direct influence on the design of this model he must nevertheless have followed its creation closely and with enthusiasm. He was certainly allowed to drive it, and there is a record of a trip he made from

*Two views of the beautifully bodied Royale roadster designed by Jean for Mr Esders, surely among the most handsome cars produced by Bugatti, or indeed any manufacturer.*

78

Strasbourg to Paris with Lieutenant Frederic Loiseau (who crossed the Sahara in a Bugatti) at an average speed of 67mph. Even allowing for the lack of traffic in those days, and having regard to the roads, this shows that Jean had clearly inherited his father's love of speed, and that the car had an impressive performance.

The construction of the Type 43 body is simple, having only one door to ensure maximum stiffness and with a minimal wood frame. Rigidity is derived from the curvature of the steel panelling. Side valances cover the chassis frame and lower the line of the body, and the louvres punched into the various panels aid cooling (perhaps) and provide cursive ornament (certainly).

The success of this body – over 100 were made – must have encouraged Bugatti to branch out into 'proper' coachwork on his touring chassis. It is here that Jean's hand and eye can be seen. Although we do not know exactly when, we do know that a special small design office was set up with full-size drawing boards where body lines could be produced in full scale, in side elevation, and at least a half section of the front elevation, which due to symmetry is enough, with the contour lines being drawn in section by section, as is the practice in yacht and ship design. The experienced body draughtsman and designer can visualise three-dimensional curvature from the rate of change of section lines, just as the map-reader can visualise hills and valleys from the contour lines of a map.

Over the next few years we can attribute a number of body designs to Jean, acknowledging as we have done in the case of his father the great contribution to the development of ideas that will in practice be made by the draughtsman who actually draws out any design. We can mention and illustrate some of these bodies:

*Fiacre-style.* Ettore had been interested in the 'razor edge', cab-like 'fiacre' body ever since he ordered one for his wife in 1911. He and Jean certainly encouraged the production of a number in the Molsheim body shop, of which the most beautiful was probably on a Type 46 chassis.

*Profilée.* Jean was undoubtedly the originator of the 'profilated' or streamlined body produced in small quantities on the 3.3-litre and 4.9-litre chassis. He raked the windscreen sharply and cut off the rear of the body vertically, in contrast to most contemporary attempts at streamlining which curved the front and rounded the rear.

*The Type 55 'Super Sport', a road-going version of the Type 51 racing car, represented the ultimate in pre-war sports cars, with a performance to match its looks.*

Jean's solution seems more in line with today's styles.

*Roadsters*. There are those who feel that the only contribution to body aesthetics made by the American motor industry is in the evolution of the roadster body of the Chryslers and Fords of the late 1920s and early 1930s. This, the cheapest model in the range, had a bench seat in front and a 'rumble' seat for two in the rear ('dickey' in English, 'spider' in French). It has been called the playground of American youth.

Jean Bugatti evidently shared the interest in this solution to the design of the sporting runabout car, as he produced first a version of the Grand Sport Type 43 (the 43A), complete with locker for golf clubs, and then a smaller model on the 1½-litre Type 40 chassis. The detail treatment is excellent, in particular the clever use of panel-beaten mouldings on the body scuttle to facilitate two-tone painting.

*The Royale Roadster*. Perhaps the most remarkable body for which Jean was responsible was on the first of the monster Royale cars which Ettore managed to sell, with a 12-litre engine and costing four times as much as a Rolls-Royce! This beautiful car was made in 1932 for Mr Edsers, a wealthy clothing manufacturer, who did not drive at night so needed no headlamps. To some this is the most beautiful body ever put on a motor car chassis – if such a superlative may be allowed. Certainly the rear treatment is very good indeed.

*Type 55 Roadster*. It was Jean Bugatti who in 1933 inspired the production of a 'Super Sport' version of the Type 51 racing car, in an available long-wheelbase chassis, just as had been done a few years earlier with the Type 35. This time he used no doors, but cut away the sides and added long, sweeping mudguards to give the car an appearance that has never been bettered in the sports car world, and which incidentally had a performance to match its looks.

*A 'Ventoux' fixed-head coupé Type 57, clearly owing much to the earlier 'profilée' body style, such as that shown on page 76.*

*Touring bodies on the Type 57.* By 1933 Jean was well in the lead, and his father left him the main day-to-day responsibility for the development of the new production car, the Type 57 3.3-litre model, which was the main production model up to the war. Fine engineer that he was, Jean was able to introduce much-needed improvements, including a one-piece crankshaft, properly lubricated; the twin camshaft layout from the Miller design, but in a simplified form; and integral gearbox with silent, constant-mesh gears; and eventually and most importantly, hydraulic brakes.

But we are here interested in his body designs. Molsheim left the production of drop-head coupés to specialists – the local firm of Gangloff, who had worked with Bugatti since 1910 – and concentrated on saloons or fixed-head coupés. Names of Alpine passes were used for some of the bodies, and we may note: 'Ventoux', a version of the earlier '*profilée*' design; 'Galibier', originally a four-door pillarless saloon and later a more normal four-door model; 'Stelvio', the Gangloff drop-head; and then 'Atalante' for a pretty, two-passenger coupé, usually fixed-head; 'Aravis' for another Gangloff drop-head two-seat model; and finally 'Atlantic' for the extraordinary 'Aero' coupé.

The Aero body appeared in 1936 in prototype form, believed to have been made in 'Elektron' (magnesium alloy) sheet, but the three that were sold used normal aluminium, rivetted along the seams. It had doors that curved up into the top to facilitate entry to the car. These bodies were produced on the Sports 57S chassis, lowered and shortened, and with a tuned engine and V-shaped radiator – extraordinary, bizarre and interesting, but not perhaps beautiful in any normal sense. Today two remain intact; the third rebuilt after a severe accident. All three are inevitably valuable collectors' pieces.

In the period up to the 1939 war the factory produced some 800 of the touring models. It also contrived, without the government assistance available in Germany and Italy, to run a modest racing programme. Initially this comprised a batch of cars based on the Type 57 touring car but with a supercharged engine and a new chassis. The body was still a two-seater, with the panels riveted together as on the later Atlantic. This car, known as the Type 59, had some success, although later, when the racing programme as a

*The Type 59 3.3-litre supercharged racing car was based on the Type 57 tourer and had modest success on a limited budget. The great Tazio Nuvolari is at the wheel here.*

whole was abandoned because of expense, the name Bugatti was kept alive in racing circles by a car or two running in sports-car races and by two single-seaters that were unsuccessful in racing classes. Better results came from splendid tank-bodied cars that won at Le Mans in 1936 and 1939. These were made at Molsheim, as those that ran at Tours in 1923 had been, but were better conceived and made. They were the progenitors of much post-war sports car racing design. By this time Ettore had retired to Paris, so these cars were wholly the work of Jean.

Jean's end came on 11 August 1939. As he had done before, he took out the Le Mans car to test it prior to the forthcoming Grand Prix at La Baule. A stretch of road was closed at each end by colleagues, but they had not bargained for a tipsy farmer on a bicycle who rode into Jean's path while he was travelling at speed, causing him to swerve and crash into a tree. He died instantly.

The war came a few days later, surrounding Ettore with yet more tragedy and forcing him out of his beloved Alsace for the second time in front of the invader.

BIOGRAPHICAL SUMMARY

1909 Born Mülheim-on-Rhine
1914 Moved with mother to Milan and then Paris
1930 Type 50
1936 Effective chief at Molsheim; 57 Tank car wins at Le Mans
1939 Died Molsheim 11 August

*One of the streamlined 'tank-bodied' cars which won the Le Mans 24-hour race in 1936 and 1939, foreshadowing the shape of many post-war sports and racing models, seen here competing at Montlhèry.*

Bugattis were designed to be driven, not admired in museums! There are keen Bugatti clubs in Britain (recently celebrating its fiftieth anniversary), the USA, Australia, France, Germany, Denmark, and Holland, with active pockets of interest in Belgium, Sweden and even Japan. These clubs encourage the use of the cars on the road, and in Britain on the racing track and in hill climbs, where they can be seen in their element.

There are also many cars in museums, with a large selection of over 100 in the French Schlumpf collection at Colmar. The Harrah Museum has a fine and well chosen selection at Reno, USA, and in Britain one of the original 1924 Type 35 cars is in the National Motor Museum at Beaulieu, Hampshire, and there are several models in the Donington Collection. Most of the better known car collections boast at least one or two Bugattis, and there are many in private hands, although these are not always generally accessible.

The remaining population of Bugatti cars today is in excess of 1600 out of a total production of about 8000.

*Very much a final fling, Wimille in the 1938 3-litre single-seater Bugatti car.*

# Acknowledgements

The publishers would like to thank all the individuals
and organisations who have helped in the compilation of
this book, and in particular to express their gratitude to
Mlle L'Ebé Bugatti for her assistance.

Illustration material was provided by the following:

*Autocar pages 56, 61*
Jean Badré *page 82*
Bugatti Family Collection *pages 5–7, 10, 13–15, 24, 28, 29,
    31, 32, 35, 48, 49, 60, 65, 69*
H. Carabin *page 77*
H. G. Conway *pages 52–55, 57–59, 61, 62, 64, 65, 69,
    71–74, 77–81, 83*
Courtauld Institute of Art *pages 36, 42*
Centro Storico Fiat, Turin *page 60*
Clive Helm *page 27*
Leviton Atlanta *page 51*
*Motor pages 9, 75*
H. Roger-Viollet *page 52*
Royal College of Art Library *page 22*
Sotheby's Belgravia *pages 15, 16, 18, 20, 21, 23, 25, 26, 31*
Strother Mac Minn, Los Angeles *page 76*
The Sladmore Gallery *pages 36–40, 43, 45, 46*
Tim Street-Porter *pages 19, 23*
M. Turner *page 72*
Christopher Wood *page 12*